Dedicated to Kathleen,
my Wife and my Best Friend

All proceeds from the sale of this book
will be donated to
The Irish Guide Dogs Association

Editor's Notes

It has been a great pleasure to read this work, as it is a greater pleasure to know this man. Though I have, over the last year, heard bits and pieces of this tale, it was with the totality of Liam writing this book that a complete person presented itself to me.

While doing the editing for this book, I made comments that Liam Lynch responded to favourably in places, and with laughter in others. But what was appreciated most was the language with which he expressed himself – the language of his own voice from his own place, that honours both the man and his readers with its honesty. He is himself in these pages, with the best and worst experiences of his life revealed. It would be a nice closing note if each of us could share with one another in so open a manner, enriching each other with the stories of one another. Give it a try.

Brigid Hurley

Table of Contents

With my Grandfather and my brothers, John and Patrick, in 1940.

Introduction

Up a quiet boreen in Gortroe, Knocknagoshel, a boreen bordered by hedgerows of fuchsia, privet, nettles, gorse, hydrangeas, ferns and roses, lives a tall, slim, blue eyed man who can spin ten foot tall stories. In mid summer, the enclosed garden abloom lies in stark contrast to the dry bog-land and uniform forestry of the surrounding town-land, which the house overlooks.

The telephone line extending from this two-storey farmhouse over the hills of Brosna and deep into East Cork was my first connection with the man who lives there, Liam Lynch - my uncle. As a child, I could instantly recognise his roguish tone and the distinctive uvular 'r' that marked his speech patterns. The weekly telephone conversations between my father, Patrick and Liam were one of the mainstays of the dinner-table conversations over Sunday roasts. Stories of what Liam's neighbours did and said, tales and lore with a twist and a sting in their tails, and yarns retold in the North Kerry dialect that was alien, yet magical to my young ears, a dialect that could make the crudest thing sound poetic.

Knocknagoshel was a strange exotic land populated by people who spoke in riddles and danced to a different tune from those inhabiting my childhood world.

The Liam Lynch of my youth has changed very little from the man I know today. He still has sparkling blue eyes, his sense of mischief and roguery has not diminished nor has his sharp tongue been blunted. He still has an overwhelmingly kind, gentle and generous nature, his reservoir of stories still overflows and his ability to probe your character and help you reveal truths about yourself operates as un-intrusively as ever. He remains a singularly empathetic man whose empathy has evolved through personal life experiences marked by darkness and light.

Liam Lynch's story is of a life of innocence, happiness, romance, learning and humour. Though these aspects reflect the core of the man, it is also the story of a life of immense personal pain and suffering, one of stoicism and acceptance, a story of profound mental strength, development and growth.

Distance and the adult instinct to protect young people from certain knowledge and experience blinded me from knowing the exact suffering and pain that Liam went through as his own sight faded. News of what Liam had done and of what he had achieved were still relayed by my father over the dinner table as I grew up, with what I regard in hindsight to be, a fierce pride. Pride, admiration, respect, and in many ways awe, define how I view Liam today. He has canoed, he has swum, he plays goal-ball, he can cook, he e-mails friends worldwide daily, he collects and trades in rare books, he makes calls to Radio Kerry, some serious, some mischievous, he speaks at public functions, he walks the roads for miles around Knocknagoshel, he has surfed waves in Louisburgh and he has made a brave attempt to climb Croagh Patrick, almost making it to the top. He is in his late 60s and he is blind.

I listened to Liam talk about writing this book and sometimes observed him go about the monumental task: dredging up bad memories, mentally filing and editing the good memories, trying to put order on his story, writing and deleting, despairing and hoping, and all painstakingly typed by him with nothing but the aid of his speaking computer. He could not scribble notes so maintaining a chronological sequence was harrowing at times to say the least, all of which makes the book a remarkable achievement.

Liam's story documents his North Kerry childhood, the social, agricultural and cultural trends and mores of that era, his love for family and nature, for animals and the land and of course his sense of place. Stories and yarns are interwoven throughout and help to reveal the characters, social values and culture of the world described. He is unsparing in documenting his failing eyesight and the consequences it had for him. The real shining light in Liam's life is, however, his wife Kathleen and it is very apt that the final words of this story reflect the love held for her and the gratitude and appreciation so deeply felt.

Like the hedgerows in Gortroe, Liam's life story contains things of beauty, flowering fuchsia, roses and hydrangeas, but it is the weeds, the nettles and briars that weave through and defile the hedgerows, and yet form an integral part of them, that reflect Liam's inner journey through hard times and the scars that he bears with fortitude.

Eanna O Loingsigh.

Where Life Began

"What we learn to do, we learn by doing"
(Aristotle)

I was born on the eleventh of July 1938, the third son of John and Josie Lynch, of Kilgarvan, Ballybunion parish, County Kerry. In the years that followed, 1939 and 1940, two more children were born, a boy and a girl. The names of my brothers were Patrick, John, Timothy and another Timothy called Tim. My sister was called Marie. Tim was named after his older brother who had died just prior to Tim's birth. My brothers were called after our father, grandfather and an uncle, with Marie carrying her aunt's name. This aunt had entered the Presentation Convent in Limerick City and her vocation was regarded as a great honour in the family. In admiration of one of Ireland's heroes in our War of Independence, my father named me in memory of General Liam Lynch.

Our family was of farming stock, living on sixty acres, operating the farm as tillage and dairy. We shared the dwelling house with my grandfather, John P. Lynch, whose authority was never questioned. I remember with fondness the influence my grandfather had in the upbringing of us children - a vital factor in those days when my parents were occupied working manually on the land. Our household was self -sufficient in its upkeep except for flour, sugar and kerosene. These were the days before electricity, piped water, radio or telephones. Bucketfuls of water were boiled over open fires, hand-scrubbing did for family washing, and few women were able to benefit from the hand-operated mangle, which squeezed the water from the clothes.

It was from this rural background that I learned to live and make friends with cows, calves, donkeys, horses, geese and ducks. My first encounter with the outer world was when I accompanied my mother in a donkey and cart on the six-mile return journey to enrol at my first National School in Coolard, Lisselton, Listowel, Co. Kerry. I was just four years and eight months and up to then had never attended a church service or a public gathering. When I arrived at the school I was astonished to see a lot of children playing, surrounded by a stone wall, and was not impressed by the man in charge. He walked amongst these children, better dressed than my father was when he attended Mass.

Early days with my mother and brother at my old home in Kilgarvan.

I did not like what I saw, which included a smiling lady, unknown to me, walking in my direction with her hand outstretched as if to welcome me. I was seated on the wall, and made the terrible mistake of catching her hair and pulling it, at the same time calling her "a dirty bottom" or worse. Obviously, I did not wish to go to school, become a prisoner of that yard, and leave behind the freedom of the fields and my friends. However, as history relates, I had no choice and spent my first day at school with my brother in May 1943.

The smiling teacher looked sterner that morning, and told me where to sit and to behave. I was thankful that she did not refer to the incident on the wall, in front of the class. I was given chalk and a slate, and was told to draw whatever came into my mind. I drew a horse and a foal as best I could and was rightly pleased when rewarded by the teacher for my efforts with a piece of chocolate. About a year later our teacher must have been influenced by divine inspiration. She decided to teach us boys, in this rural school, how to knit. It would be hard for the reader to understand that a knitting needle with a knob on top was unavailable at the time. She realised this and took the advice of an old lady, who told that in early days, they used a large feather from a goose's quill, instead of knitting needles. We shaved the plumage off the feather, leaving a little piece of feather to prevent the thread coming off the end, and also to protect our eyes.

When we returned to school the next week to start our knitting lessons, all but one boy had these quills. This boy's father, who was considered a handy man in the locality, had made needles for him from the spokes of an old bicycle wheel. Our teacher supplied wools of many colours, which I believe were shop leftovers, although there would not be much of that around at the time.

First steps were taken on how to learn plain knitting. We stuck it out for about a week, white feathers and bits of scrap wool, doing what we considered girls work! Finally, our teacher examined our work and the class came to a full stop. She had lost her usual composure, and burst out laughing at our efforts. I remember well the tears streaming down her face in sheer enjoyment. However, I do not believe these lessons were a complete failure, because years later I was able to sew in a button on my pants, and darn the heel of my sock. At this stage I began to like and respect my teacher and today look back fondly on her teaching skills. I believe the education of any child starts during these tender years and I regard my time spent with this teacher to be of vital importance. I believe our teacher paid as much attention to each pupil as she did to her own son, who was also in my class. On my last day in her class she recounted the pleasant time she had spent with all of us, and told us she considered it all a pleasure. And so I completed this early part of my education.

My parents, grandfather and my brothers in 1940

TUMBLEDOWN

"The roots of education are bitter, but the fruit is sweet"   *(Aristotle)*

However, I was moving up and considering myself a big boy, as I would now be getting my education from the senior male teacher. I gradually became aware that he was inflicting severe punishment on his students but most of them seemed to be well able to take it. They appeared to me to be grown men.

On going into third class, I received my new books, copies and jotters and was allowed home early, as our teacher was starting the new term the next day.

On leaving the school, the wind had become very strong with occasional severe gusts. Due to my slender frame, when I reached a high rise of ground on the roadway, I was blown across the road into a clump of briars. I looked around in horror, as my new books, of which I was so proud, lay scattered around the ground. I gathered up the books as best I could, but noticed that some were torn by the wind and soiled by the earth. On arriving home I told the story of how I was so scratched and so late, but did not tell my parents about the books, of which I was so ashamed.

On arriving at school the following day, our teacher, who had seemed so friendly the previous day, now appeared more strict and abrupt. All the students were requested to stand to attention when their names were called in Irish. We were then informed that where we now stood and sat would be our class place for the next twelve months. We all accepted this discipline without any question.

We were then asked to present our books and to stand by our desks while the teacher inspected them. Explanation was demanded of me as to the condition of my books. I made an effort to answer, but the words choked in my throat, as no other boys had a similar experience. My teacher produced a cane and cut it across my open hands, saying as he did so, "I will get you to speak". The more he caned me, the more frightened I became and therefore I was unable to make any explanation or excuse.

I was in a deep state of resentful emotion, as he caned me until I cried. The schoolroom had become silent during this exhibition, although the caning continued until I cried out in horror and fear. I was lead from the classroom into a hallway and was told to grow up and to stop moaning. The door to the schoolroom was closed and I was left alone in that hall for some time. A little while later my first teacher passed, exclaiming, "My poor pupil! Liam, what did you do to deserve this?"

I believe this incident prompted my nice teacher a short time later to take a teaching post in another school, thereby removing her own son, from the likelihood of a similar cruel experience.

I may have been sometimes responsible for the anger of my teacher, as I was a dreamer and unable to concentrate on my lessons during class. As a means to counteract my daydreaming and to hold the attention of the class, our teacher developed the following method. He would get us to circle around the blackboard and then write a mathematical problem on it. He would ask one pupil to start solving this problem. At any stage during the lesson, another boy could be called on, to continue where the first boy had been requested to stop.

I can now vaguely remember the teacher putting the chalk into my hand and asking me to continue, having removed the previous pupils work from the board. I quickly became aware of the danger of the situation and tried as best I could, to make a quick mental calculation of the sum on the board. The next thing I remember was receiving a clout of his open hand across the head. I staggered, falling helplessly to the ground, but recovered quickly only to receive a vicious slap on the other side of my head. I was not so lucky this time, as my head hit a pointed end of the skirting board and blood flowed down my face. When he saw this, he made me go to a nearby stream to wash away the blood. The impact of the cold water on the wound soon stopped the bleeding and I returned to take my place in the class. At this stage, all my respect for this teacher vanished and I developed an intense dislike and hatred for this man, and for most people in authority.

When I had arrived home in the evening, and having eaten my dinner, I was usually asked to take tea and bread to the man working in the garden. How I loved this man's carefree way of life. It was he who taught me how to make a catapult, how to trap rabbits and catch fish. By leaning in over the bank of a stream at mid-day when the fish were resting, I would catch them unawares and with one quick flick of my hand throw them over my shoulder on to the dry ground. I have fond memories of him telling me to take salt in my hand and when seeing a bird or a rabbit, to shake salt on its tail and then it would remain my pet forever. I did this for months, until I noticed the twinkle in his eyes and realised he was only joking me. When drinking his tea he always shared his bread with the dog and made a *"toisin"* of paper in order to give the dog the last drop of tea. How I laughed with boyish delight, as he allowed old Shep to lick his face unrestrictedly. I would remain helping him until dusk fell. He would then request me to go to the boggy meadow and round up the herd of milking cows, and drive them to the pump field where he was waiting. I loved gathering the cattle from the shadows of the trees and bushes. They would have been lying down for the night in a particular form or arrangement, and I sometimes rested on the land and felt the heat their bodies had generated. If one was missing, I could always locate it by watching out for its breath coming out of a clump of rushes in the frosty air. What a beautiful sight.

When the cows had drunk sufficient water from the trough, we drove them on to the roadway, where they took their time and walked home at their own pace. The man or the dog never intervened, but sometimes the cattle would stop, lick their bodies, give a disgruntled look and then continue their slow walk home. For our entertainment and educational needs, my father would read and analyse poetry for us. His favourite at the time was Thomas Gray's "Elegy in a Country Churchyard". As I walked along the road on that beautiful evening, I recalled to mind the opening verse from that poem, and there and then, before my young eyes, I saw for the first time in my life, the true meaning of poetry in motion.

ELEGY IN A COUNTRY CHURCHYARD.
(Gray)

The curfew tolls the knell of parting day,
The lowing herd winds slowly o'er the lea,
The ploughman homeward plods his weary way,
And leaves the world to darkness and to me.

"Leaves the world to darkness and to me" took on a different meaning altogether for me later on that night.

When we arrived at the farmhouse, I would make my way to where the light from the kerosene lamp was shining out into the darkness. Inside, my mother would have prepared supper, but I would not eat until my friend the workman would have joined us.

Before retiring for the night, my grandfather would recite the family rosary, in which all the family joined together in prayer.

Later on during the night, I would wake, about the same time, in terror, thinking my screams had awakened the household. I would wait listening for any sound, but could only hear the deep sleep breathing of my brothers. These nightmares occurred night after night, at about the same time, and I became very frightened of the stillness and the darkness and sobbed violently. My father came to the room and asked me why I was so terrified, but I could not explain to him that it was the terrible beatings I was receiving at school that were causing the problem. The only thing my Dad could do was to take me into his bed, where I would sleep contentedly in his arms until morning. I believe that these beatings stole from me much of the precious years of my boyhood. I have often asked myself if I could forgive this man, but to do so, would be to try to convince myself that this never happened. In my lifetime, I believe that these beatings created in me a deep distrust and suspicion of people in authority. The beatings and insults have haunted my mind for the greater part of half a century. They always seem to return at a vulnerable time of my life, usually at the time of a death in the family, or that of a close friend.

When I returned to school after the summer vacation, I did not participate during the breaks in any games or fun. I usually stood alone in a corner, and perhaps the boys thought I was sick or delicate because of my gaunt look, due no doubt, to bad eating habits and poor quality of sleep.

At the end of term, when classes were being changed, I thought like some of the other boys, that I would remain for another year in my class. However, I was surprised when told to take my position in the next class. At this stage, my teacher had stopped beating me, and I was making some real progress. However, I noticed that he was dishing out the same severe punishment and insults to the young boys in my previous class. It was obvious to me that he was of the opinion, that if he controlled and instilled discipline into the young lads he would have an easy time for the rest of their four-year period in school. It was very hard for me to receive such punishment, but a lot more difficult to watch these young boys going through what I had already suffered.

I was seated at my desk one morning when I noticed an approaching shadow in the hallway of our school. I looked towards our teacher who looked surprised. There was a gentle knock on the door and in walked the school inspector. He nodded good morning, greeted us pupils in Irish and then proceeded to have a friendly conversation with our teacher. He examined the roll books, and as I was absent on many occasions, he called on me to answer why. The inspector said, "Liam why have you been absent so often?" I was very surprised at the respect shown to me, in calling me by my name. I explained that I had been sick on many occasions. He then asked my teacher if I ever had a doctor's certificate, and in answer, he whispered into the inspector's ear, "truant". The inspector then asked me if I ever heard of the word "truant". I replied, "no, sir". He replied "ok", and indicated to me to resume my place in the class.

He spoke briefly to the class about the structure of a written composition. He asked if we understood these examples and the class responded, "Yes". He then asked us to write a composition about the life and death of a marauding fox. I wrote my composition as humorously as I could, tying in the fox's life with that of a roguish neighbour, who was known locally for his daring and not so daring exploits, as "Fox Kennelly". He began reading my composition, staying with it for some time and muttering to himself in an inaudible voice. He then examined the rest of the class, stopping at times to request some pupil to read his work for the benefit of the class and the teacher. Finally, he returned to me and asked if this was the only copy I had. I replied, "Yes", as I had lost the other one. He then examined my copy in detail concentrating on my work in Irish. I was surprised when he asked me if he gave me the price of two copies, would I promise to keep them in good condition. I said I would and to my surprise, he gave a shilling, much more than their cost. When he asked me if he could take my old copy in exchange, I quickly agreed. He took it in his hand to the end of the room, where I was sure he would burn it in the open fire. To my surprise, he placed it in his case and zipped it up, shook hands with the teacher, said good-bye to us and walked out of the school. We got the rest of the day off as a reward for our good behaviour, but my teacher never referred once to the incident of the copybook.

During the summer vacation, I felt a lot better emotionally and started organising the local boys to prepare for the St John's night bonfire. With my father's permission, we gathered old shoes, sticks, peat, and furze bushes until we had a big mound at the crossroads. I had hoped to outdo the other groups, especially by having a larger bonfire than the one organised by the boys one mile away, at Ballyline cross. However, I was outdone by the boys who had a much larger bonfire, around which they danced and sang, "puddings and pies for the Ballyline boys", and chanted in reference to us, "mail (meal) and bran for the Kilogram clan". I have no idea of the origin of this practice, but locals had claimed it was there from pagan times. The church in Ireland failed to stop this practice, so they gave it a saint's name (St. John) thus allowing it to continue. This custom has largely died out, but how exciting it was then to see all the bonfires ablaze on the hillside at approaching darkness.

We started coming together again in playful groups and claimed the headland of my father's garden as our territory. We would be quite safe there from some bad-tempered bulls, and this area would not be used until the end of harvesting.

It was a beautiful spot, surrounded by hedgerows with lots of nesting birds who had a plentiful supply of food in the garden. We removed the scrub from an old fallow tree and this became the group's place for discussion. In a corner of the garden we set up a platform, on which we acted out our own homemade plays and dramas. Some of the boys also sang, whilst I mimicked the local politician. For this part of our show, I would have my grandfather's hat and glasses, and I must have been the first barefoot politician for many a day! To applause from the boys, I promised them longer school breaks and free tickets to Duffy's circus, which only visited our big towns annually.

We were sometimes joined by the local girls, who played the game of shop-keeping. They had found discarded pieces of delph, the best of which they displayed on their shelves.

Then one girl had a bright idea of pulling a turnip from the garden and smashing it on a stone until it was reduced to soft pulp. They did the same with carrots and other vegetables from the garden, into which they squeezed blackberry juice. Then they decorated it with berries picked from the hedgerow. We boys were made to queue up and pretend that we were paying for this "food". How I laughed, as the girls lifted their chins and condescendingly asked us, "How can I help you?" without recognition of any brothers, cousins or us.

As the summer progressed, we planned our football games here and sometimes slept in our hideout there until my mother called us home for tea. It was about this time that I had started to read, understand, and love the poetry of Patrick Kavanagh. He must have had the same experience in his boyhood as I had, for he composed the following poem from which I now quote.

PEACE. *(Patrick Kavanagh)*

And sometimes I am sorry when the grass
Is growing over the stones in quite hollows
And the cocksfoot leans across the rutted cart-pass
That I am not the voice of country fellows
Who now are standing by some headland talking of
turnips and potatoes or young corn
Of turf banks stripped for victory.
Here Peace is still hawking
His coloured combs and scarves and beads of horn.

Upon a headland by a whinny hedgerow
A hare sits looking down a leaf lapped furrow
There is an old plough upside down on a weedy
ridge
And someone is shouldering home a saddle-harrow
Out of that childhood country
What fools climb to fight with tyrant's Love and Life
and Time.

The happiness of our house was disturbed for a short time, by my brother Patrick leaving for boarding school for the short term, September to Christmas. I was disturbed by his going, because apart from being the eldest of my brothers, he also provided good leadership, which I admired. On the day he departed, there was a great sense of sadness in the whole family, causing my mother to be very silent and my father failing to do his usual evening reading to us. My parents and neighbours all hoped that Patrick would follow his Uncle Patrick's footsteps and become a priest, but he had other ideas. Before retiring to bed that night, my grandfather addressed my mother saying, "Woman, there are many bad things in the world, but your son going to the seminary in Killarney is not one of them".

When my brother returned at Christmas, I noticed a big change in him. He did not join in our games and he was reading more advanced books.

Christmas Eve was always a wonderful time in our household, with plenty of cake, lemonade, and if available, a good-sized mackerel for supper. There was always great ceremony around the lighting of the Christmas candles, which were placed on windowsills; this was a sign of welcome for everyone. The youngest person in the house was my sister Marie, who lit these candles, as was the custom. As each candle was lit my grandfather would carry one into the room in which a member of our family had at one time died, or was absent from the house. We joined in prayer at this stage for the well-being of the absent. There was not much made of the visit of Santa in those days, as he had very little to go around.

On Christmas morning, the whole house would be awake at dawn, as we helped our father and mother to tend the cattle before breakfast. We would travel the three and a half mile journey to Mass at Ballydonoghue Church, which in the horse and trap, took a good hour. Many people walked this journey and it was pleasant seeing the lighted lanterns, as the Mass goers made their way across fields and down boreens.

There would be many families on the same journey on their horse and traps and some of the horses would neigh to each other. The first horses would slow down and late arrivals would catch up, thereby forming a closely-knit cavalcade

Each cart in this procession looked very alike, except for the strange looking woman placed in the middle in one of them, with her cart being drawn by a thin, hungry looking piebald pony. She was one of the travelling families, known locally as tinkers, due to their ability to make farm utensils from tin.

As the cavalcade moved past the "Sailor Connor's" house, a splendid animal placed his head over the back door of our trap, breathing heavily, allowing my brother and I to warm our hands on his hot breath. I looked straight into the pony's eyes and I detected a twinkle of amusement, as I think he knew what he was doing for us!

The church was lit with candles only, which gave a lovely sense of Christmas to the ceremony. The only motorised vehicle at the church was the property of the parish priest, who after Mass gave a short Christmas message and wished everyone a happy Christmas and a prosperous and healthy New Year.

On our way home, my father asked us children to walk the last mile or so to allow my mother

My father and mother, John and Josie Lynch

time to prepare Christmas dinner. There was little movement at this time of day, except for the swift low-flying blackbirds along the hedgerows, as the thawing frost startled them, causing a lovely rippling sound amongst the decaying leaves. As we came around a bend in the road, we were only a few yards away from the tinker's camp. The lady with the piebald pony was brushing down her pony with a fist of straw. She was unaware of our presence, until my younger brother called out to her, asking if she had a goose for Christmas. She turned sharply and on seeing the two of us, laughed out happily at our presence. I had never seen a person so thin and her lovely smile was darkened only by her few remaining decaying teeth. She then asked us did we belong to the family living in the two-storey house beyond the crossroad and we answered, " yes". We talked for a little while, about things that I cannot remember today, except for one question: would we remain in the area when we were adult men.

I noticed that she wore a small cloth-like purse on a leather thong around her neck. What she did next makes for the happiest

Christmas I ever remember. She emptied the money from the purse into her hands, and then she divided it equally between my brother and me. This seemed to me to be all the money she possessed, which made her gesture all the more wonderful. I retained one small coin from this money, which I have to this day.

CHRISTMAS MEMORY (Liam Lynch)

There as young boys, at the crossroads we stood
On that lovely Christmas morn, now so long ago
Joy in our hearts, smiles of happiness on our faces
Receiving the gift of love, from the queen of
travellers
The precious memories that would linger
And which we would cherish for years and years,
and forever.

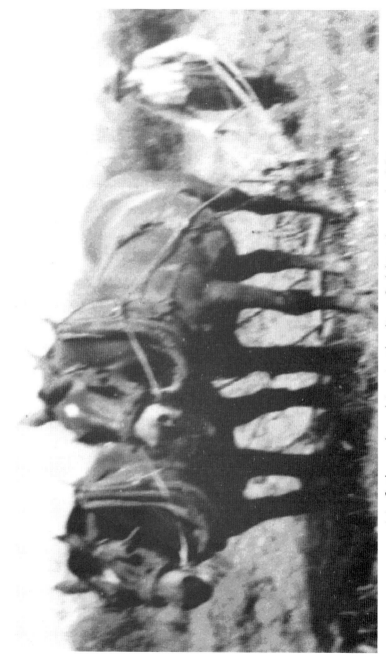

My father ploughing in the line field in the early fifties

Growing up on a farm always kept me close to nature. Sometimes, there would be an animal that died, which had to be buried, with the help of the neighbours. I can recall coming from school one evening and seeing a newborn foal in the field. I looked with sheer amazement at the size of the foal, running beside its mother and wondered where he could have come from. When I entered the field to get a better look at him, he stared back at me with curiosity. The next thing, the mother became excited and chased me back out of the field the way I had come in. The foal stayed close to his mother and was looking under her neck, as if he enjoyed the incident. All requests to my father and the workman, as to where the foal had come from, were greeted with big smiles! I laughed when the men told me that he came out of his mother's tummy. I could not believe it, as I could not see any large opening there. It was only later, when I saw a cow calving, that I understood the process of birth.

At about this time our collie dog, Shep, went missing and failed to return home. Eventually I found him dead, in a local bog, where I think he died quite suddenly, chasing a hare. When I first saw him, he looked to me, in the distance, as if he were alive. When I finally came close to where he lay, limp, I put my arms around his neck and wept uncontrollably over the loss of my friend. With the help of a neighbouring boy, we brought him home in a donkey and cart to our playground in my father's garden. It must have been a strange sight, not to see one able-bodied man helping us boys digging the grave. Usually the men would have dug the grave and buried the animal. All our friends, girls and boys were at the burial. To his memory, we built a small mound of stones above his grave. It is over a half a century since Shep's burial, and the little mound of stones to his memory is still there to the present day.

It was about this time, that many homeless men travelled the roads of Ireland, usually staying at some local house for the night. They were mainly British ex-service men , who had fought in the First and Second World Wars. When the news spread that one of these men was staying locally, the neighbours from the surrounding area would gather to hear stories of his adventures, some very true and some a little "airy-fairy". They usually had their own food, which consisted of tins of beans, coffee, and hard biscuits, which they sometimes shared with us girls and boys.

One of these men, known to us only as "The Rebel", called to our house, at about the same time every year, usually staying for only one night. If the morning were wet and windy, he would remain on until it cleared, usually passing the time by reading some old newspaper, before resuming his journey to God knows where. I can recall quite clearly his last visit to our house, sitting on the old armchair, with his eyes closed, singing for me my favourite song, "Gold and Silver days". Some of the words from that beautiful song are still in my mind and they have helped me to recall some lovely memories from that period.

Gold and Silver Days (Traditional)

"As I am sitting by the fireside
And turning back the years
I can hear my mother singing in the morning
As she scrubbed our shining faces
And then packed us off to school.
Oh! Too soon those days were over, without warning
Oh sing me a song of our gold and silver days
Days filled with memories of life
Not a penny to our name we were happy just the same
In our gold and silver days.

We gathered at the crossroads on Sunday's afternoon
Then we danced the sets and polkas, at the Royal
Through the years they all have scattered, but my friends are loyal and true
So sing me that song of our gold and silver days
Days filled with memories of life
Not a penny to our name, we were happy just the same
In our gold and silver days".

It was the following summer that my grandfather became seriously ill and although my parents cared for him, he eventually went to the district hospital in Listowel. He failed to respond to medical treatment because of his old age and was sent home to end his days.

Shortly before he died, he called me, my sister, and my brothers to his bedside, gave us some money, and asked us to live honourable and decent lives. It was some time afterwards that he became confused and asked me to take him to the local race meeting at Ballylongford. I was heart-broken that I could not carry out his wishes, but I promised to do so as soon as he got well. He just smiled in response.

Early in the morning on the thirteenth of October, I was awakened by my parents hurrying to my grandfather's bedside. When I got to the room, my mother was kneeling by the bedside, and in a calm voice, was reciting the divine praises. She ended suddenly, and called to my father, "Daw has just died". We all gathered in the kitchen and my father put the alarm clock on the table and said to us children, "you will never forget the time your grandfather died". It was a quarter past seven. He sat for a time at the end of the table in deep meditation and for the first time, I saw him break down and cry. My mother took control of the situation and we all joined in reciting the rosary. When the prayers were recited, my father regained his composure and was able to continue work in the farmyard. About an hour later, neighbours gathered around to help and, as is typical, allowed the family time to grieve.

My grandfather, John P. Lynch, was a very strong character who always wanted his wishes to be fulfilled. He requested that when he died, his body should not be taken to the local Church, but instead should be taken directly to the graveyard for burial. This was against Church rules at the time, as they wanted the body reposing in the Church overnight and a funeral Mass the following day. His wishes were fulfilled and there was a very large funeral from the house, with all sections of the community represented. The last time my father talked to me about my grandfather, was on Christmas Eve that year, when we cut holly for the Christmas decorations. He explained to me that this first Christmas in over ninety years my grandfather was not in his own home. He looked very sad gazing into the distance, saying, "Never forget Daw and always remember him and pray for his soul". In conclusion, I believe that I was privileged to have spent the first ten years of my life in the company of my granddad, as he was the perfect role model for me and the rest of our family.

During the late forties and early fifties tuberculosis was sweeping the country, causing the deaths of many people, both young and old. A government minister, Noel Browne who suffered from the ravages of this disease, laboured valiantly to establish sanatoriums and health centres, such as the one at Foynes, County Limerick. To control the spread of this disease, the government instigated an animal health programme, as they believed the drinking of unpasteurised milk and the eating of beef from affected animals, was causing the spread of TB.

My father being a very progressive farmer and mindful of the health of the people, was one of the first people to have his dairy herd tested for TB under the new scheme. Only one animal reacted positively, and on the advice of the veterinary surgeon, she was destroyed and buried on our farm. Our family was heartbroken, as Daisy was a lovely and affectionate cow and had become quite a pet. Ours was a dairy herd and as such were expected to be with us for a long time. Each animal had a personal name some having been inherited from previous animals or owners.

The vet arranged with my father, to have Daisy killed on a Friday evening. The workman made a halter from the horse's reins and placed it around Daisy's head. She walked after him very gently, her head just bobbing slightly up and down to the motion of her body. They halted at a gate, entered a field known as the middle meadow, and went to the corner of this area, where the men had already dug her grave in the rich alluvial soil beside the stream.

I watched this scene from the upstairs window of our two-storied farmhouse. The vet pointed a gun at Daisy's head. I heard the bang, but Daisy was still standing. I was just about to shout that they could not kill poor Daisy, when she slipped forwards on her knees, keeled over, and died. It was a few days later that my friends and I visited her grave and found the farm implements used for the burial still standing by the grave. It was the custom at the time to leave such equipment at the grave, either for humans or animals, as a mark of respect. We boys thought that the grave was untidy and that it needed improvements to make it look like a human grave. We raised the earth about four inches and smoothed it carefully until we achieved a nice rectangular form. I organised a chain gang to the nearby river, from which we removed flagstones that we placed upright around the grave in a kerb fashion. One of the boys excelled at the work and interestingly enough, became a stonemason in later life.

On completion of the work, we stood by the graveside, with the silence broken only when one of the boys picked up the spade, and with reverence, wrote the name "Daisy R.I.P." and underlined it.

It was early the next spring, that I crossed the fields and climbed on to a very high fence, in order to view Daisy's grave. What I saw astonished me. The grave-site was completely covered with swaying bluebells. Everywhere else around was just rough grass and weeds.

I called my friends to witness the lovely flowers on the grave, and we all agreed that God indeed must have cows in heaven.

It was years later, that I realised that the bluebells grew on Daisy's grave, simply because the earth had been disturbed, allowing the bulbs to blossom a little earlier than usual. Bluebells had always grown here a little late in the spring.

I believe that growing up in rural Ireland with such friends, and my association with animals, has developed me into a more caring and understanding individual.

It is now more than half a century since Daisy had to be put down. Sadly, most of the old ways and customs have long since died out. Most of the boys who were there with me on that evening have long since emigrated and some have died, but life must go on. I walked with my brother to the corner of that meadow recently, and as I stood there remembering the days of my boyhood, the following lines came to my mind.

DAISY (Liam Lynch)

Flowers bloom in the springtime on Daisy's grave
Daisy is also the name of a beautiful flower
It grows all round here midst the wild grasses and
weeds.

Bordering this lovely scene in shades of white and
gold
Flowers bloom only to decay, but they always blos-
som again in spring.
Will Daisy return like the flowers?
Yes-
She had many calves.

I returned to school in September of the same year, following the summer holidays. I was now in fifth standard following the class change-over in May. The teacher had resumed strict discipline and was preparing us for the following year's examination, the Primary Cert. By now, I did not mind the corporal punishment so much, but did wish he would refrain from the insulting name-calling. I deliberately with-stood the punishment of the cane and contin-ued to mutter to myself an old mantra that I had heard from our farmhand. It was: "sticks and stones may break my bones, but names will never hurt me".

On our way home from school, we usually encountered the long acre cow and a group of eight to ten donkeys. When the donkeys saw us approaching, they turned away, forming a circle with all their heads in the centre. They resembled a rugby scrum, as they circled in a clockwise motion, their legs kicking back at us, their tails wagging and some of them breaking wind in defiance of us! We boys formed a circle around the donkeys, waiting for a break in their ranks. I spotted a break and moved in very quickly, grabbing a grey donkey over the nose with my left hand and placing my right hand on his mane. I was on his back in a flash. The ranks broke and to my delight, my donkey charged with great speed, back in the direction of our school. A local man working in a field had observed all this commotion and started to cheer me on. He stuck his spade into the ground, hanging his cap on the handle and started calling out. "Even money bar one, four to one the field". All of a sudden, the donkey turned in the direction of a whitethorn hedge, stopped suddenly, catapulting me into the thorns and briars. The make-believe bookie roared out laughing, "Gone at Beechers' Brook"! I recovered just in time to see the donkey running away, shaking his head from side to side and braying loudly, "he ha". It was a good lesson for me, as it took me over a week to remove all the thorns from my body!

I've always had a great love for donkeys, but especially for one little foal on our own farm, which we called "Folly". My brother and I had turned this little foal into a complete pet, which followed us both everywhere we went. Hence the name "Folly". The local girls did not appreciate Folly as a companion and tried in vain to chase him away. He would turn back, but then rejoin those kicking legs, springing from side to side, taunting them. His mother and himself were great rogues and we had to be careful when eating apples or a slice of bread, that they would not snap them out of our hands.

When we were saving hay in the west meadow, Folly would run into the meadow at lunchtime begging for scraps of food. In order to keep the tea warm for the workmen, my mother put it into an earthenware pot and covered it with a woollen cosy. Being the devils we were, we went to drink it through the spout of the teapot. He became an expert at this trick and you should have seen his ears lying back like a contented rabbit, as he sucked the last few drops!

On our way to Mass one Sunday morning, I noticed Folly a few hundred yards behind us. I did not alert my father and mother to this situation, as they were deep in conversation. When my father noticed Folly, it was too late to turn back. He smiled and said, "Boys, you will be dealing with this problem yourselves". As we stopped our horse and trap to tether it to the halting place, he allowed my mother and sister to go uninterrupted into the church. Then he requested my brother and I to do likewise, but the donkey followed us. The men standing by the wall laughed and joked, asking, were we taking our brother to Mass. We were very embarrassed, until one stepped out, grabbed Folly and said, "This fellow was as close at the birth of Jesus as some of those jeering mens' ancestors". This stopped the laughing and he put the donkey into an out-house close by the local pub, opposite the church.

My brother and I did not object when, the following year, my father sold Folly to a local businessman, who would keep him as a family pet.

The station mass was a bi-annual event of great importance in our town land. This practice started at the time of the Penal Laws and has continued uninterrupted until the present time. It was always an important day for children, as they would be given a free day from school. These station masses were held in the homes of the parish and were usually in a seven-year cycle for each homestead.

Food was scarce during the war years, but all the neighbours contributed something in the way of supplies, thereby helping to make the day a success and a wonderful feast. I often helped the neighbours at these preparations by white washing gate piers and outside gable ends and farm outhouses. I was never allowed near the main part of the farmhouse, as this job was always reserved for the local handyman. I never expected any reward for my work but, come the Listowel races I always got a few bob from the householder.

On the morning of the station, I called to the house of a friend, who lived at the crossroads next to our house. I liked this man, a senior citizen, as he was the same person who had a few months previously intervened on our behalf at the church gate during the donkey incident.

When I entered the house, I was surprised to see him admiring himself in a mirror, which he always referred to as the "looking glass". When he faced me, I saw for the first time in my life, that he was wearing an expensive dark-coloured hat. He asked me how I liked the look of it; I replied that I thought it was a little too big for him. "Ah sure", he replied, "the story could be a lot worse. If it were too small, then I would not be able to put it on my head at all". As we walked to the station house, he explained to me that he had found the hat lost on the roadway and all efforts by him to locate the owner had failed. He smiled and said, "I suppose at this stage, it is a case of finder's keepers".

On entering the house, we were warmly greeted by the parents, their family and relatives. The woman of the house accepted my friend's hat and placed it on the hallstand for safekeeping.

The owner of the house and his wife, who were always well dressed for the occasion, remained just outside the front door until the parish priest, his curate, and clerk arrived. There was a tone of reverence in their voices when they greeted the priests, and the man looked a little proud as he introduced his reverence to his neighbours. As the parish priest removed his coat and hat, he would be heard to say that he was pleased the farmers had a good harvest, and that there was a good price paid for milk and an excellent market for cattle. One man, who was standing near the back door and out of earshot, was heard to say, "The good man knows what he is talking about and I promise you there will be an increase in the station dues announced this morning"! He proved to be correct.

It was almost noon before the priest had finished reading Mass, hearing confessions and collecting dues; some were still referred to as oats money. Some of the well-dressed men were then asked to join the priests at the table for the morning breakfast. No woman, no matter what standing she held in the community, was ever asked to join this select group. The rest of the men were asked to leave quietly and go to an outhouse, where they were served generous amounts of whiskey and bottled Guinness. I joined this group with my friend and it was fascinating to watch them drinking, sitting on three-legged stools and even some lying out full length to their hearts content on the body of the donkey and horse carts. Sometime later, my senior friend asked me if my father would allow me to accompany him for the afternoon to his hotel. It could be called anything but a hotel, as it had no electricity, running water or toilets. It was usually frequented on Fridays by old-age pensioners, who sat around a big open fire, drinking, dozing or recalling stories from the past. When I asked my father for permission to accompany my friend to the pub, he said OK, but warned me not to be out of the way for my farm jobs in the evening. My friend then asked me to go into the house and ask the grandmother to give me his hat as quietly as she could. I waited outside the door as instructed until she came out with the hat under her apron, saying "I know what that old fellow is up to, he wants to escape to the pub without his breakfast". She then placed two pieces of fruitcake into my hand, saying, "You will need it before the day is out".

We were soon on our way and I was surprised how sprightly my old friend could walk. We stopped briefly at the gate of my parent's home, where he asked me to go to the shed and get two Bengal blankets, a term he used to describe a jute bag. He used this bag as a cushion when he sat on a fence while smoking his pipe.

We were just seated comfortably in the pub, when the old bar attendant came in a hurry, saying to my friend, there was a well-dressed man looking for him outside the door. How all the men laughed when he said, "boy, go out and see who wants to meet me without an appointment". When I got to the entrance door, I was surprised to see a very agitated looking priest's clerk pacing up and down the footpath. Seated in the front passenger seat was the parish priest who had read Mass at the morning station. He looked anything but happy. My friend became very alert when he heard this news and moved quickly to the entrance of the pub, to be greeted by a very angry priest, who said, "So it is here you are at last, you villain". The priest lowered the window of the car, at the same time saying, "Is this my hat?" "My God it is father, and there must be a terrible mistake. I will be out in a few seconds". He muttered to himself, "Fair exchange is no robbery". As they exchanged hats, I heard the priest saying, "I will take the smile off your face and that of the old lady back at the house before the end of this year". "My God, father", he replied, "I am sure the good old lady had nothing to do with it, it was just a terrible mistake and I am sorry". "I do not believe you", he said in a stern tone, "my hat is two sizes smaller than yours and you must have noticed the difference". My friend leaned forward so that he could look the priest straight in the face. "Come to think of it father, I noticed a difference which surprised me. It was all the people who lifted their caps and hats in respect to me as I entered the village today". The priest asked the clerk to drive away quickly before he would lose his temper. My friend winked and smiled broadly at me, saying, "That should keep that old fellow thinking for some time to come".

When we returned to the bar, my friend ordered lemonade for me, a half pint of Guinness and glass of whiskey for himself - the whiskey he always referred to as a chaser. We were not questioned about the incident on the street, and regular conversation resumed as normal. For the rest of the evening, I did odd jobs for the men, such as buying groceries and checking that their transport had been fed and watered. I usually bought groceries from the far end of the town, as the shop owner always rewarded me with a little money. The men in the pub always did likewise and of course, I always looked forward to these trips.

Later on in the evening, my friend said, "It's time to take you home, boy". Of course I knew that his excuse for my being there was so that he could leave the pub earlier in the evening. On our way out of the village, we encountered the Garda Sergeant who was just leaving the barracks for the evening. Normally my friend would have deliberately avoided him, the priest or the schoolteacher. However, when they came face to face, my friend raised his hat, genuflected and exclaimed, "What a fine looking man you are sir, in your uniform". The sergeant stared at us one to the other repeatedly and fiercely said, "If you two do not get out of town, I will lock you up for the night". I was not frightened because I detected a sly old smile on his face as he turned away.

About a mile out of town, my friend stopped in front of what appeared to me, to be a vacant farmhouse. He took his pipe from his mouth and staggering gently, pointed the stem at the house and complained bitterly of the part these people played during the Civil War. As we walked away from the house, I asked him to explain which side they had taken during the conflict. He replied, "I do not know, but they took some side and that's what made the difference".

About a mile from home, he stopped and entered a field, to water his pony, a polite countryman's term for having a piss. Opening the gate seemed to take forever, with him cursing the late blacksmith and any person who had had a part in even hanging the gate, but, he seemed to have no problem closing it. When he finally emerged on to the roadway, he cocked his eye at me, saying, "Take that smirk off your face and get home the road before me, you rascal".

When we arrived at our house, he took a purse from his pocket and fumbled until he got some money from it. I reluctantly accepted the coins, as he and his friends had compensated me well during the day. "Take it boy", he said, "for it will be the last day I will be needing your help, as I will not be walking to the post office, to collect my pension in future. Cousins of mine have agreed to collect it once a fortnight, and drive me to the nearby town of Listowel for my groceries". He was a little sad as he said goodbye. I watched him as he walked away, until he disappeared over the brow of the hill. He seemed to have aged a lot over the last month or two.

Looking back on those years, I think my friendship with these men taught me how to appreciate and enjoy the company of the elderly. I will finish this part of my story, by quoting from an old Irish proverb, "Their likes will never be here again".

At school when we were preparing to receive the sacrament of Confirmation, the teaching of all other subjects stopped, except the study of Christian Doctrine. For some days ahead, the teacher looked very concerned and said that if every boy made an effort to achieve, he would not inflict any corporal punishment during instruction. The results were excellent.

Then one day we had a visit from our Parish Priest, to examine us on our progress. He did not dwell too much on what we had learned, as every boy seemed to have the answers at hand. Instead, he advanced to stages that we had not yet touched on, as an indication that we had a long road ahead. We were all disappointed to receive the harsh judgement and insults that followed these unforeseen questions.

In an angry voice, he called us "blockheads", "sods of turf", "goats" and other terms I have forgotten. Occasionally he reached out and pulled our hair, chucked us about and referred to some as "blackguards" and "tramps". The class was devastated and angry. It was later that we christened this Priest "the monster". He did have a remarkable likeness to Boris Karloff, who acted as Frankenstein in the movies.

One week prior to Confirmation, he examined us again and, without any encouragement, stood in the doorway and said, "I will see you all in church on the fifth of June".

When the Priest had gone, our teacher sat in the centre of the class and said, "I suppose some of you boys think I am the devil from hell, but would any of you exchange me as a teacher for him?" Most hands were raised and everybody called "no". However, I did not respond, I just stood motionless, thinking, "Surely, two wrongs never make a right"?
On returning to school after summer holidays, I entered my final year at sixth standard. Teaching was very intense during this period,

and the severe punishments and insults had eased off considerably.

One day we were standing in a circle reading a story from our English textbook, when as usual, my concentration was lacking, and my teacher noticed this. He called on me to continue reading where the last boy had stopped. This was impossible, as I did not even have the correct page open. He snapped the book from my hand, opened the correct page and with his index finger pointed to the exact place where I should read. One of the boys started making funny faces and gestures to me behind the master's back. The teacher was resuming his seat, but turned around quickly and caught me laughing. He was already reaching for his cane, as he hissed, "I'll take the smile off your face, you blackguard". Gently he took hold of my wrist, and held out my hand and a sly smile crossed his face, as he raised his stick above his head. I saw the cane coming with force and quickly pulled my hand away, allowing the stick to crash onto the desk, sending shock waves along my teacher's arm and sending splinters from the smashed cane all over the room.

I saw the danger as he came towards me

and quickly backed away to the far end of the room, but he still pursued me. I calculated that I was fleeter of foot and that if I could get between him and the free standing desk, that I would make it to the outer door and safety, before he could catch me.

The anger in his face was frightening, and this helped me to make a dash for the door. I escaped just in time to hear the door being banged behind me. He followed me into the open yard and shouting loudly declared me banned from the school, saying that I should never attempt to return. Shortly afterwards, he came outside with the boy who admitted to making the funny faces, and banned him also. The boy told me that he'd felt sorry for me and admitted to the teacher that he was responsible for the happenings. This boy was of very good character and only minutes after the incident, gently knocked on the school door and waited until our teacher re-emerged. The master, on seeing him, repeated to him that he was banned, but the boy brushing past him, said, "I understand sir, but I'm not going without my books", nor did he. Repeated efforts later to get this boy to return to school all failed.

While still standing in the yard, I calculated that I had only three more months left to end of term and therefore decided to take a chance and return to class. I resumed my place as quietly as possible and the teacher just ignored me. He continued to do so for the remainder of the term. On the day of our summer holidays, which was my last day at school, the master in a friendly gesture was giving out sweets to the class, but just before he got to me, I picked up my school bag, placed it on my back and without comment walked out of the door, to what I considered freedom. However, as I have stated, freedom was not to be, as those beatings and insults continued to haunt me for the next half century. One must remember that corporal punishment was legal and widely used throughout the educational system at that time. Thankfully, for teachers and students alike, this practice ended officially, as late as 1982.

MOVING ON

"Crafty men condemn studies, simple men admire them, and we wise men use them."
(Francis Bacon)

Some months later I sat the entrance exam at the Listowel Technical School and got a final place in the A class.

On the first day at school, the headmaster introduced the class to our new teachers. Our subjects included mathematics, woodwork and English. I was pleased with the curriculum. We were encouraged and never punished for failure. Discipline was strict and was dealt with in a firm, stern and fair way, by the headmaster. Should a pupil continue with bad behaviour, a letter would inform his parents. I had only been brought before the headmaster on one occasion.

The pre-Christmas exams ended just before the holidays. On returning to school in the New Year, I was interviewed by my woodwork teacher regarding my future career. His name was Eamon Kelly, who in later years became a famous actor and storyteller in this country and overseas. We spoke in Irish, and when I told him that I expected to become a farmer like my father, he smiled and said "Of all the boys I have interviewed, you are the most likely to do what you say." I had great respect for this man and we became good friends, a friendship that lasted for most of our lives, only ending on his death at a great age some years ago.

I loved my time at this school, as much for the knowledge that I was gaining, as for the fun we boys were getting from the athletics. During this period, I had grown much stronger and healthier, and was very proud when chosen as left corner back on the possible football team.

My parents were very hard working and my father was up at dawn doing the farming jobs. This was the case with all farmers at this time in Ireland before any machinery was used on Irish farms. It was not unusual to have a hard day's work done by nine in the morning. As I began to be more aware of the hard work my parents had to put in every day, I tried to help as best I could with the chores in the morning.

Frequently, before going to school, I took the milk delivery to the creamery. This meant I was often late for school.

At that time, unknown to me, my father was suffering from a medical problem. An ulcerated growth close to his ear was a cause of worry to him and my mother, a worry they kept from us children until hospital treatment was needed. Until that time, I slowly got more involved in the day-to-day running of the farm, while my father took a necessary back seat.

I was late attending school one morning, when I met the woodwork teacher in the corridor. He asked me why I was so late; I replied in Irish that the wind was not helping me, rather than explain that my father needed my help. The actor in Mr. Kelly came out immediately, as he raised himself to his full height and, with eyes closed, said, "I thought the wind only interfered with ocean going liners Liam". Later on during the day, he explained that if I was late again, I should have a covering note from my parents.

Of course I was late again and, when I gave him the hand-written note, he studied it very carefully and looked sympathetically at me and told me should I be late again, no explanation from me would be necessary.

By the month of May, my father's condition necessitated hospitalisation. This was the end of my school days, as I had to remain at home to help my mother run the farm. Most of the responsibility rested on me, as my older brother was teaching in Galway and my brother John was attending University in Cork. My younger brother who showed a talent for farming was, unfortunately, in hospital recovering from acute appendicitis.

We were heart-broken when my father was sent to hospital, but understood when the doctor explained that, following surgery he should make a full recovery. Even though my mother heard the reassurances, she still carried a deep worry. Thankfully, a couple of weeks later, my father did return home, but on doctor's instructions was told not to do any farm work until the wound healed completely. This took a couple of months and what a wonderful day it was, when we were all working on the farm once again side by side with my father.

School Days Over

A few more years in a classroom desk
Seemed the unwritten rule.
Then I met a lass near Corridan's cross
And turned my back on the school.

(Johnny Morrissey, Gortroe, Knocknagoshel).

One evening, while working in the field preparing the ground for spring wheat, my father asked me if I would consider staying at home and help on the farm. I consented and that was the end of my school days. From then on, I would be expected to share some of the responsibility of the day to day working of the farm. With instructions from my father and the help of my older brothers who had returned home for the holidays, we completed the harvest in good time that year. All the neighbours co-operated, helping each other out, a practice known as "cabhairing". It was a great neighbourly tradition. For instance, if you had a meadow of hay fit to wind and it looked as if it might rain, any neighbour that was available would rush to your assistance. Often after the hay was secured, a football would be introduced and a lively game would ensue. It was startling how far some of these lads could kick this ball with their bare feet. Therefore working on the farm became a very enjoyable experience for me. Selling cattle with my father, or buying bonhams (piglets) at the markets and fairs was something I loved to do, as I considered myself a bit of a wheeler-dealer.

One evening my father asked me if my brother and I would consider taking two heifers and sell them at the fair in Listowel. I told him I would be delighted to help, but was not sure if I could manage the dealing without him. He explained that he was getting older and it would be of great assistance, to have us go to the fair and do the cattle dealing. I was very pleased that my father could place such confidence in me. I was feeling sad that my father was unable to be with me and was close to tears when I felt my mother's gentle reassuring hand on my shoulder, saying, "Sorry Liam that it has to be this way, but it will all work out for the best, you'll see".

On the eve of the fair day, my younger brother Tim and I rounded up the cattle and drove them to a field at the far end of our farm, known to us as the West Meadow. My father always used this method, as it gave us the added advantage of being near the main road and a half-mile nearer to the market town of Listowel.

On the morning of the fair, we were up long before dawn. When we had eaten a hearty breakfast prepared by my mother, my father helped us to get on the road for our big adventure. He said to take care of ourselves and wished us the best of luck. Before leaving, my mother sprinkled us with holy water, a common practice in those days. My brother, who had remained silent up to then, smiled and said "Sure it's not to America we're going Mom!"

With the help of torches we located the cattle and drove them onto the road. My brother drove the cattle and I walked on in front, closing any gates left open by careless farmers.

About a mile further on the road, we met up with some other farmers on their way to the fair. With their help, we arrived in good time at the square in Listowel town, where the open fair would take place.

I stood the heifers at a prominent place in the square, close to the Bank of Ireland. My father had told me that this was a good sales point, as the cattle dealers would be passing by on their way to lodge or withdraw money from the bank. From this vantage point, I watched the square filling up with herds of cattle driven by their owners. There were many kinds of cattle on view, old cows with long horns, cross-raggy bulls and calves in creels drawn by horses and donkeys. The men were dressed in all types of clothing, such as old Garda pants; ex-army boots and jackets, some even wearing discarded womens' hats and bonnets. The hats were purchased from a Knocknagoshel man, who had opened a second hand clothing store in Charles St. in Listowel. He had bought them at a closing down sale in one of the big stores in Dublin and charged one and sixpence for each hat.

As I knew this character fairly well, I was sure he made a reasonable profit in the transaction! Most of these clothes were bought from tallymen, a local name for traders who sold second-hand clothes on the street at markets and fairs. Most of the farmers carried the useful ash plant in their hands, or well tucked under their oxter, when not in use. Most of the young men wore their caps back to front, as it was the fashion at the time.

I was rudely awakened from my dreaming by the squawking of crows from the nearby rookery in Gortinard Wood. They were announcing, in their own way, that it was dawning for day. I checked the time on the old clock situated on the steeple of the Protestant church; it was just about to strike six o'clock in the morning.

It must have been the recognised signal for trading to begin, as the square seemed to come alive to the sound of men shouting at men, as they tried to make deals between the owners of the cattle and the jobbers. The man next to me had refused several offers from the same jobber for his cow. "I'll make you one more offer and that will be the last," he exclaimed. He spat on his hand, at the same time asking the farmer to hold out his hand. The buyer again spat on his hand and quickly slapped the farmer's hand. This was a sign that the bargain was made and sealed.

Many buyers came, inspected our heifers, and enquired where the owner was. When I told them that I was selling the cattle, they would all say, "I cannot buy and sell them for you, get some help young fellow". One strange man said that I would get no bid for my cattle, as I was asking far too much. I am now sure he was acting as a go-between to break me down in the price for the next buyer. It was then that I noticed a tall well-dressed man approaching me. He was wearing a broad rimmed hat, brown crombie coat and brown-laced leather boots. He also carried a full-length yellow cane. He examined the cattle carefully, sometimes standing back a little to have a better look at them. He then asked me the reason why I had charge of selling the cattle. I explained that my father wanted us to get used to bringing cattle to the fairs and that this was our first time doing so. He said he would not like to see young lads wronged and for that he would give us the top price for the heifer. "There will be no bantering, I will write a price on a ticket and if you accept, I will remove the cattle immediately and pay you by cash or check in an hour's time at the Listowel Arms Hotel".

I was about to accept what I considered a good offer, when I heard a loud voice saying, "Stop the sale". I looked around and recognised the man who had interrupted the bargain. He was a relative on my mother's side, whose name was Jack. The buyer was white with anger as he approached my cousin, saying, "What right have you to interfere with this sale?"

My cousin didn't reply. The buyer continued, his voice shaking with anger. "I bought these cattle in an open fair, and there is nothing you or anybody else can do to stop me taking them". My cousin Jack met the angry dealer's look with a steady gaze, at the same time picking up some cow dung from the street with his bare hand. With the dung, he marked the letter 'x' on the left hip of the two heifers saying, "That's one thing you forgot sir, the cattle are mine now and I'll pay their full value and a few quid to boot also". Then, to my surprise, Jack started to wipe his dirty hand on the clean tail of one of the heifers, at the same time keeping a steady but amused gaze on the stunned face of the cattle buyer. I was then beginning to realise that, without my cousin's intervention, I would have been conned into selling the cattle at a price well below their value. The onlookers applauded Jack. Their actions did nothing to calm the situation, as it provoked an angry and hostile response from the cattle jobber. He moved forward and confronted my cousin, saying, "I'll take you to court and you will have to pay my expenses and that of my helper". Jack replied in a soft voice, "You can try that too". The cattle dealer sneered and shouted, "I could buy you and your kind out with what spare cash I carry in my pocket". This statement seemed to anger my cousin and he replied, "I could probably do the same, if I took advantage of young fellows on their first day at the fair". It looked as if a dangerous confrontation was about to take place when the cattle dealer whipped of his coat and hat, handing them to his companion.

He threw his cane on the ground and, brandishing his fists in the air, he called out to

Jack and said, "If you were a man, we would settle this argument in the old-fashioned way". "Let the best man win", the onlookers shouted, at the same time encouraging Jack not to let his side down. Jack moved a little closer to the dealer, saying, "Why don't you leave quietly and go about your business"? The dealer only sneered at this suggestion, saying, "Come out and stop hiding behind these young fellows". He then addressed the onlookers, saying in a loud voice, "I think we have discovered a big coward here".

As quick as a flash of lightning and, before the onlookers had time to respond, Jack had whipped off his coat and hat to reveal a broad-shouldered man with a thick head of black hair, strong muscled arms and hairy hands that almost reached to his knees. The keen eyed cattle buyer must have been the first to notice this as he backed away quickly, saying, "You can have the cattle, as there won't be much luck with them". "I did not buy them heifers for that you coward", Jack said, "but if there is any such thing as luck in this world, it will come to those who act in a decent and honourable way". Jack then addressed the onlookers, saying; "Go about your business, as you will get no free drink from me". He was referring to the fact that, if the cattle jobber had won the argument or fight, he would have stood a drink or two in the nearby pub.

It was now mid-morning and most of the trading had ceased, as most of the cattle had been either bought or sold. The workmen from the Council were busy brushing the street and washing it down with buckets of water. My cousin called me aside and asked me to tell my father that he would call to our house and pay for the cattle the following Sunday. There was little change in his personality since the encounter that morning, except I noticed his eyes were shining more brightly under the brim of his hat.

He told my brother and me to come more often to the fairs and watch the deals being made and broken, saying that it would be the best education we could have for life. "Liam", he said, "tell your father if he wishes, he can buy back the best one of those heifers at the same price as I paid you for her here today".

Just a few yards from where we were standing, a man had started playing sacred music on a piano accordion. He then started preaching about the evils of our time and warning that we should all prepare for the second coming of Christ. He attracted some attention, but very little from the country folk, who seemed more interested in meeting friends and going for a pint of stout in the nearby pub. He gave a long talk on the Good Samaritan. I smiled when I heard a man to say, "and who in the name of God is that"? I was completely engrossed in the gospel preacher, when I felt a slight tap on my shoulder. It was my cousin Jack, saying with a smile, "If your father buys back the heifer Liam, you should name her the Samaritan!"

Months later we paid a visit to my cousin Jack, so that my father could thank him personally for helping me at the fair. Jack was a bachelor, and lived in an old-fashioned farmhouse which he kept very clean and neat. We were greeted warmly and he asked smilingly, "How are you getting on now, young fellow?" He retired with my father for a private conversation, while I prepared the bread and tea and boiled the kettle on the open fire. After the tea, we went to a field to look at the two heifers that Jack had bought from me at the famous fair. He insisted that my father buy back the best animal as he had promised, and took him out of earshot to arrange the price. Included in this deal, was my father's purchase of a small beast as a comrade for the heifer. We drove them on to the roadway and Jack said, "Give them their head boy, for I'm sure that heifer will be home long before you", and so she was. I remembered Jack's advice on the fair day to call her the "Samaritan". This we did. This heifer proved to be a wonderful producer of calves and milk and became the foundation of our own breeding herd. Interestingly, my brother who inherited our farm, still has descendants of the "Samaritan" that make up the main part of his dairy herd.

Later as a marriage gift, my father and mother gave us a present of a beautiful heifer, descended once again from the "Samaritan". My new bride and I also called this heifer the "Samaritan" and she in turn became the foundation of our dairy herd.

A working "Samaritan"!!!

Many years later my wife Kathleen, who was a most capable farm lady and quite used to the buying and selling of cattle, broke down and cried the day we sold the "Samaritan" due to old age.

A rare picture of a steam powered engine from the 1940's

In the coming months, I settled into the daily duties of farm work. In the spring of that year, I was busy sorting the potatoes - larger ones for our own use and any surplus to be sold in the weekly market held on Friday in Listowel. I was so busy working that for somtime I was unaware of a voice calling me, saying, "Hello, young man, you look very busy". When I looked around, I was surprised to see a young girl standing on the fence fifty yards away. I did not recognise her as being one of the local girls; they would have known my name. She was dressed in a beautiful white dress, and her jet-black curly hair was tied up with a red ribbon. I walked towards her, and then noticed through the budding sallies and blackthorns, a little piebald pony and side trap. I knew then that she was one of the travelling communities, whose father had recently camped in a disused quarry field, a few miles beyond the Blackwood cross. We talked, on the fence, of things common to young people, such as dancing and what school she had attended. In answer to a question from Bridget, as to whether I would emigrate when I got older, I said "probably". She smiled and said, "My people have no land, money or houses and yet none of our people leave the country". I admired her dress, and she explained that she got this dress from a wealthy shop owner, whose daughter had died in a tragic accident.

The custom of travelling people is that clothes and garments from a deceased person should be burned. They had accepted the dress, only because it had never been worn. It was then that we exchanged names and I was pleased to call her Bridget. As the eldest girl in the family, she had the honour of being the first to wear the dress, because it would be handed on to her sisters and then their cousins in turn. She smiled and said, "Liam, by the time I will get a chance to wear it again, it will be in tatters". Her father warned her not to go gaging (begging) at houses where there were no children or young people. "I'd like to take home something for the evening meal though, Liam. Would you ever get me some of those lovely potatoes from the garden?" I filled the bucket until there was hardly room for my hands to hold the handle. I then went to the roadway and tipped the bucket of spuds into the body of her cart. When I looked at Bridget, her dark eyes were beaming with excitement and I asked her as politely as I could for a kiss. She laughed and said, "Be off with you Liam", but the words were hardly out of her mouth, when we were in each other's arms, kissing. Out of the corner of my eye, I noticed my father further on, coming home from the creamery, observing our little bit of fun. He moved on quickly as if he had not seen us.

After she said good-bye, Bridget jumped on to her cart, catching the pony's reins and with one quick call, she cried out, "gwon gwon" as the travellers do. I watched Bridget disappear and I never met her again in my life. Everything was quiet at home during dinner until my brother and his pals started saying, "Liam kissed the tinker girl", "Liam kissed the tinker girl"! I was blushing with shame and sweat was pouring out of me. I glanced shyly at my father and saw a very sympathetic face shining down on me. He turned to the others saying, "You've had your fun, enough now. I will be having a word with this fellow later on in the day".

It was later that I explained to him what happened with the girl on the road. He told me that he had no objection to me meeting girls, but that I should remember that, even if I was the finest looking man in Ireland, a travelling man's daughters would have nothing to do with me. He then explained to me that the travelling people have their own code of behaviour and would only marry within their own community. He advised me to stay clear of that camp, or they would give me a bit of a hiding.

My life slid by quickly when I went dancing with my friends to the local halls. It was important for me as a young man to interact with the outside community, as most of my friends and the young people were emigrating to America, England and Australia. Those early dancing days I spent at the local parish church halls. The one I most enjoyed attending was the one located at the village of Asdee. I liked the atmosphere in this hall, as the girls were pleasantly rural and the electricity had not yet reached this lovely village. The lighting was only by Tilly lamp, which had to be primed, even in the middle of a dance. The cloakroom of those days was only a few cup-hooks on the wall at the far end of the hall. Everyone just threw their coats into a heap and found them again at the evening's end, by a process of elimination.

One year, our cloakroom was filled with turf by the local priest. This fuel was to keep the sacristy in the nearby church warm before morning Mass. In the dance hall there were only two long benches, where the girls sat until the dancing commenced. The boys grouped together inside the door, standing, talking and at the same time observing the girls.

When the dancing commenced, most of the girls were on the floor dancing. The shy boys who were unable to dance, took possession of the vacant seats and when the dancing finished the girls sat on the first available knees they could find. This would be the first encounter with females for most of these young local boys. The music was supplied by Michael Jones, whose band arrived in his open lorry used by him for transporting turf and delivering sand from the strand at Ballybunion, which would be used as fertiliser by the local farmers. If a fight threatened during the dance, Michael would form a ring with the stronger boys and the two troublemakers would be subdued, rather than face embarrassment in front of the girls.

Some time later, when electricity came to the hall, the Tilly lamp was sold on to a local householder. I remember dancing the "Siege of Ennis" in the new bright light, when some bucko reached up and turned off the switch. In the dark it would take some time to find the switch, so that we could resume dancing. It was this very darkness that enabled me to make my first date. As we were very shy, we quickly disappeared unknown to our friends. It was later that I took her home, seated on the crossbar of my bicycle and was surprised when she expected me to be able to carry her on the crossbar to the top of this steep hill, whilst still cycling. In my manly pride I would have broken the chain on the bike, rather than fail in the attempt. I now believe that this girl was teasing me and it must have been an effort for her not burst out laughing, even when I had got to the top, half dead.

At this stage it was late at night and I had to cycle the last part of the journey alone. Depending on weather conditions, I would take the long way by the Blackwood cross, or the near way through the place known as the Glen. Boyhood stories had reminded me of strange happenings in the Glen, such as the Banshee's cries being heard when there was a sudden death in the area, or a hurling match being played by strange looking men in moonlit fields. I would be scared to look left or right and was pedalling like the devil, when I heard a strange eerie whistling sound coming from the bog. I ventured one look and saw a very ghostly apparition, standing only about ten yards away from me. There was no sound, but I knew there was a real presence here. My hair stood up on my neck and sweat poured from me and if I had pedalled fast before, I now had wings. I arrived home with the fear of God on my mind and was too frightened and ashamed to tell the story to my family.

Several months later, as I was cycling with friends on the same road, we heard the eerie sound again. But with company, I was much braver, and we stopped to investigate the cause. The eerie sound was caused by the wind blowing through strong needle grass and the ghostly shape was of Carroll's magnificent puck goat standing still in the moonlight observing us!

Display of new weaponry at Ballymullen Barracks, Tralee 1961

From left: Bill Bridgeman, Tarbert. Johnny Flahive, Michael "Fonty" Stack, Tommy Joe Lynch, Dave Nelligan, On Ground Michael "Drops" Enright, and yours truly, all from Ballylongford.

Fórsa Cosanta Áitiúil
Local Defence Force Days

"I vow to thee, my country - all earthly things above - entire and whole and perfect, the service of my love."

(Arthur Cecil Spring-Rice)

One friend, with whom I cycled all over the locality, asked me if I would be interested in joining the F.C.A. - that was the local defence force. I consulted with my father, who not only considered it a good idea, but also gave it his approval. I joined the force in 1955 and was very pleased that I was able to interact with boys and men from all over North Kerry.

This volunteer force had a branch in most villages in rural Ireland. It was based on a command structure and ours was the fifteenth, located at Duagh, Listowel, Co Kerry. I did most of my arms-drill, marching and training at the Eddie Carmody Memorial Hall in Ballylongford, under Corporal Bill Bridgman of the regular army. When he was satisfied that I was fully prepared, he sent me on for basic training to Collins Barracks, Cork City. I arrived there on the third of December, nineteen fifty-five, aged seventeen years, a real raw recruit. I was presented with a 303 rifle, a mug, a dinner-plate, and a knife, and shown to my room in block seven. I was sharing a billet with thirty other men of the same age. We were all instructed to keep our beds and area clean and tidy, with all blankets and sheets folded perfectly with the blue stripe showing to the front, ready for daily inspection at nine a.m. Our own personal inspection of clean boots, pressed uniforms and cleanly shaven faces, had taken place already at seven a.m. after the bugle reveille call.

For the first three days, the marching and drilling was intense and my feet became sore. On the fourth day, before being out on leave, we were called to a medical inspection and lecture. We were ordered to undress, stand in line and be inspected by a doctor and a female army nurse. This was my first time being undressed in front of any woman. To add to this humiliation, the doctor told us of sexual diseases, which I never knew existed. We were warned to avoid the girls who congregated around the main gate on pay evenings, as they would be very free with their favours in exchange for our money. I became very fright-ened when he said that if we had any sexual contact with any of them, we were to report to the orderly and have medical attention. He explained this would mean being cleaned out with a glass syringe. I must have registered shock, for he then smiled and looking straight into my eyes said, "You will get the same favours from any girl from your own area, if you learn how to play your cards, Sonny Boy". This was strange news to me, and I did not like what I heard or the way he said it.

Some nights I ventured out to explore the nightlife and entertainment of Cork City. I always walked the route by Patrick's Hill to the City centre. From the top of Patrick's Hill, I liked to observe the thousands of lights and listen to the muffled rumbling sound of the movement of the cars, as they made their way through the City. I visited the cinema and eventually found one to my liking. It was called the Savoy. The cheapest seats were at the very top and this meant climbing hundreds of steps. I always arrived early before the films, to listen to the huge organ, which rose up from the basement area and played folk songs and popular music.

A guard of honour for Scoil Réalt na Maidine 1959

In charge of our the guard of honour on this market day, was my good friend, Michael Whelan

The organ was played by Fred Bridgman, and after playing, the organ would be lowered out of our view, which could only be done by electric hydraulics. I was always amazed at this performance and liked it as just as much as the films. It was great entertainment on its own. The words of the song were projected on to a blank screen and it was marvellous listening to the singing coming from all areas and levels of the cinema. It was during these sessions that I met a lovely girl with a marvellous singing voice, who always seemed to sit beside, or near me. We chatted and exchanged names and Marie permitted me to hold her hand but, only during the showing of the film in the darkness. She explained that her mother was two rows behind us, so hand holding was not permitted during singing time, when lights were up and bright.

I remained on at Collins Barracks for a week, completing my training and Marie became my first city girl friend. I was to meet her each year when I returned to the Barracks.

When I returned home, I rejoined my unit for further training, which included rifle practice at Ballydunlea training centre. The training must have been successful, as I was sometimes chosen as a section leader during army manoeuvres. I went on to Command competitions and served in Fermoy and Kilworth. One night I was asked to remain after drilling, to discuss the possibility of accepting an N.C.O. course, which I would complete before Christmas nineteen fifty-nine. I agreed and commenced the course in early December that year. This course proved much tougher than I had imagined. It consisted of night manoeuvres in bare feet, with voice command training, that would mean we would be heard and obeyed from quite some distance. Our general conduct and personal appearance was of utmost importance. We were under constant observation to ensure that standards were high.

Three evenings prior to our completion of the course, an officer visited our billet. We were informed that as potential corporals, we had passed with flying colours and that we'd be presented with our stripes before returning home. Our trainee sergeant asked me if I would like to join the regular Army, as the training I had received would enable me to progress further in the force.

As usual I met Marie on St Patrick's Bridge and we went to the Assembly Rooms to see a film. We talked and I explained my future plans, which might involve becoming a member of the regular Army. Her voice became very alarmed at this prospect and she exclaimed, "Liam, the Army is no place for a young man like you. Remember, you have seen only the best side and how would you like it if you were not free to return home to civilian life this weekend?" As we walked, she said sadly, "I will not be here to meet you the next time, as I am going to England to train as a nurse". I immediately saw the truth in what Marie said. It was then that I made up my mind that I would not join the army.

It was a sad but romantic parting, as we watched the boats moving quietly on the River Lee. I took her in my arms and asked permission to walk her home. She wouldn't let me, saying, "Times are changing, Liam and it might not be safe. Men in uniform would not be welcome in my area". It was then she kissed me good-bye, turned swiftly and walked into the distance, without looking behind. I never again met Marie.

In the morning I received my pay and gratuity for completing the course; I went to a smart store and bought myself a new sports suit. With my uniform packed in a case, I stood in this outfit, talking to friends, just under the National Flag Pole. Our training officer, who had envelopes in his hand, approached us. One contained an application form and a photo-copied description of a uniformed man working as a security officer at Shannon Airport. The officer informed me that one of the letters was a recommendation from my training sergeant for this career appointment. My father and I discussed this matter at length and after con-sideration, he asked me to investigate the pos-sibilities further. He advised me to make an appointment with the staff recruitment officer at Shannon Airport and that he'd accompany me as support.

Assurance

"I had nothing in my mind but the interest of the people"   (The author)

I was successful in getting the interview with the management, but in the meantime a retiring official approached me from a Life Assurance Company, and asked if I would be interested in taking up his post. I knew this man's reputation was good, so I asked him for an interview so that further details could be ascertained. I was successful in getting the job. This opportunity meant that I could combine farming with my parents and still have an independent job. Apart from a salary, there was the added prospect of earning good commission for sales and for securing new business.

I asked the manager, why he had chosen me. He answered, that I was well known among the young people and had contacts and friends in the G.A.A My family were also well respected in the farming and business community. After a fortnight's training by a supervisor, I was accepted, and started in my new career.

Being short of money, I began travelling to work on an ordinary pedal bicycle. This was my only means of transport. My day usually started at seven a.m. I would ride to the far end of Tarbert parish, ten miles away. I chose this routine because the milking would be finished and the children would be gone to school, leaving the women in the house free to relax and take a break. Of course I was offered tea and accepted, thereby getting to know the families better and of course, this was good for business. This proved a good method, as come evening, I would be very tired and would have finished near to home. I did very well in the first six months and was third in my district for acquiring new business.

Through working hard and with overtime, I had saved some money and bought my first new car. It was a lovely Volkswagen Beetle, which cost one hundred and eighty pounds, which included tax and insurance for the Year. I was very excited about this little car, ZX 2071, as I was the first member of my family to own a car. As I got to know people through this business, I developed contact with senior citizens, for whom I managed their death policies.

One day on my travels, I was told that a local man had reached the age of seventy, which was the qualifying age for receiving the old age pension. I knew this would be a good time to approach him with a view to taking out an Assurance Policy. When I entered his yard, he was busy preparing straw and scallops for thatching the roof of the house. I asked him if he was interested in taking out a Life Policy and he replied "Of course, but I'll have to obtain my father's permission." I was surprised at this answer, so I asked where I could contact his Dad. I am sure he saw the surprise on my face, as he smilingly pointed up to where his ninet-four year old father was busily thatching the roof!

As I became more experienced in the Life Assurance business, the people trusted me with their savings and sometimes I even lodged and withdrew money from the bank for them. I also drew their old age pensions and delivered gro-ceries to the more remote households, when on my rounds. It must be understood that these people had very little transport and usu-ally had to rely on the pony or donkey and cart to get to town, and so my car and weekly visit became important to them.

There was one widow who lived in a very remote area and lived almost hermit-like. She had not allowed anyone inside her home for years. She always had the correct amount of money for her payment, folded inside the Assurance book, which she handed through the door, which was slightly ajar. In an effort to break down her resistance to me as a visitor, and out of curiosity, I requested that she would make me a cup of tea. There was a lingering silence until she replied in a cold voice, "Go away about your business, I don't want you". I replied, "You have not refused me the cup of tea yet, have you?" She paused and said, "My place is so untidy, that I don't wish to have anybody into the house. I am so lonely and not good company either". I promised that I would not stay long, that I'd not look at the condition of her house and told her that I badly needed that cup of tea. The conversation ended and, after a pause, she opened the door and allowed me into her home.

When I finished drinking the tea, she asked me to call more often than once a month, and to make it a two weekly visit. The next time I called, there was a big change. The house was tidier; she looked brighter and had the tea ready for me on the table. Over time, we became friendlier. I listened to her problems about living alone and how she had come to this state in her life. I was very pleased when she asked me to collect some groceries for her. I was to pay for them and she'd reimburse me on delivery. This friendship was a rewarding experience for me and, I hope, for her, as so many lonely people need only the hand of friendship to improve their lives.

On another occasion, a well-spoken lady asked me to drive her to her home, which was on my way, and I agreed to do so. Arriving at her house, I said "You are the only house in this area in which I am not doing a business call." I then asked her if she'd like me to explain the benefits of a good Assurance policy to her. Her request was to insure her husband without his knowledge. I filled out the proposal form for her and paid particular attention to his state of health, which she assured me, was excellent. I then asked her to sign the policy form. Some months later, I delivered the policy and enquired about her husband and family. I was shocked and alarmed when she replied, "As you know Liam, his heart is not good and he is lying in bed as usual".

I took her payment and prayed to God that this man would not die for at least two years. My prayers must have been answered, as the sick husband out-lived his wife by many years.

Now that I had a car, my social life improved immensely and I went far outside my own district to films, dances and plays. I was earning good money and was well able to pay for my girlfriends' nights out. Aware of the impression my job created, I gave great attention to my appearance and bought my clothes from the outfitter in Tralee town. Things were looking up and very bright indeed and, at twenty-one, I thought the world was my oyster.

Grá

"To see her is to love her, and to love but her forever,
For nature made her what she is, and ne'er made another"   (Bonnie Lesley)

One night I attended a local ball, where one girl would be chosen to represent the area at the Rose of Tralee Festival. Like all the young men around the stage, I too was admiring the contestants, but one particular girl took my eye. I was not surprised when the judge announced that the same girl, Kathleen O'Connor of Knocknagoshel, was the unanimous choice of the selection committee to represent the area at the festival. As she was awarded the winner's sash and gold bracelet, I quickly moved to the gangway, where all the contestants would emerge from the stage. As she descended, I put out my hand and offered her congratulations and said, "I had chosen you from the moment I saw you". She smiled softly and said, "Thank you, kindly". I quickly asked her to have a mineral drink with me after the celebrations and photographs were finished. She stopped, and looking me straight in the eye replied, "Yes, I will join you later". Kathleen joined me as promised and, after some refreshments, we danced late into the night to the wonderful music of a touring showband. On our way home, I asked Kathleen if she would meet me again; she said yes. There and then I vowed that in the weeks and months to come, I would do everything possible to influence Kathleen to become my permanent girl friend.

During the months to come, Kathleen and I travelled the scenic parts of the country and in this way got to know and understand each other. Sunday night was special, as I'd collect Kathleen and take her dancing to the Central Ballroom in Ballybunion. The music by Maurice Mulcahy's orchestra was excellent. In those days there was absolutely no trouble or disruptions, fights or arguments, even though there were about two thousand young people in attendance. There was great excitement when the Victor Sylvester Orchestra came to Ballybunion. It was a special treat and the dancing could go on to until three a.m. Like hundreds of people of our age, we all walked the streets and made friends. We did not go drinking, as licensing laws in those days prohibited pubs being open on Sundays. However, there was a fair trade done, unnoticed by the Gardai, for every one knew the buckos who would open the back door. The publicans always kept a watch out in case of a surprise Garda raid. One dear old lady who was known as "feach amach", peered out the door, and remarked that there was little police activity and suspected that the raid was imminent. To make sure that the coast was clear, she popped on her slippers and went up the street with the excuse that she would buy a loaf of bread. With the bread tucked under her arm, she was making her way back to the premises, when out of the shadows of the doorway an elderly Garda appeared and asked her, "Are the customers hungry as well as thirsty tonight, Jenny?" There was no raid, but Jenny took the hint and we all disappeared out the back door, as quickly and as quietly as possible.

Kathleen and I loved dancing to the strict tempo of this Orchestra and always waited until the dancing ended. Of course we occasionally slipped out during the evening and strolled hand in hand along the moonlit Ballybunion beach. I will always cherish the memories of that wonderful wide-open shore and the moon inflicting charm of the sea.

Over the next few months our friendship and love became firmly established. During Christmas of 1962, the enormous and unusual snow drifts that swept Ireland managed to separate us for many weeks. Of course at this time, telephones were very few and far between and, where they were available, had only a very limited daily service of three or four hours. Even postal deliveries were stopped in hilly and inaccessible areas such as Knocknagoshel, so that for a period I had lost all contact with Kathleen. Fortunately, my home parish was not so isolated in the snow and I happily received a letter from Kathleen. I laughed when I opened it and read, "Dear General". It was the first time she called me that and I wondered why.

Her letter explained that her brother, who was a Garda, was to go to Listowel on business and as he had chains wrapped around the wheels of his car, he was capable of getting through the snow. The idea was that if I could get to the dance-hall, she'd also be able to get there, with her brother's help. She said she would meet me outside the Bargain Stores in Charles Street. While Kathleen was putting her coat in the cloakroom, I entered the main body of the hall and noticed a young girl, dressed unsuitably for the cold weather and therefore looking blue and frozen. However, I noticed her lovely beehive hairstyle and wondered how many hours she'd spent preparing for this dance. The band was playing a Samba and I asked her to dance. As we went around the floor the blood came back into her face and she looked happier. I think she was very grateful for being taken off that seat and warmed up. Just as the dance was nearly finished, I saw Kathleen standing at the side, looking intensely at the girl and myself. As an explanation, I told Kathleen the reason why I asked this girl to dance. Later Kathleen asked how long I had known this girl. "Just tonight", I replied. She smiled and said, "That was a very nice thing to do Liam".

As the night wore on, the intense cold penetrated even the dance hall and it was strange to see our breaths as we danced. This hall would usually be crowded, but on this night there were only a small number of couples in attendance. The players in the band looked frozen until they decided to come down and join the dancers

The bandleader introduced us to a new dance that night called the Congo Line. One of the dancers, who gave the impression of being proud, became the leader of this line and his actions amazed us all, with his head bobbing from side to side, arms and legs flying, with everyone following on in single file behind him. Still acting the clown, he led us all round the hall, on to the stage, into the cloak rooms and out the front door on to the street, around the street and eventually back into the hall again. By this time everyone was really warm. We took the opportunity to leave early, as Kathleen had to return home with her brother to Knocknagoshel.

As we walked away from the dance hall the town was completely quiet. Nothing could be heard but the howling of dogs in the direction of Gortinard wood. The night was sharp and clear and there was a beautiful moon that looked as if it belonged to the town itself. The icy street glistened with frost and we could hear the band start up again. It was then I asked Kathleen if we should risk a waltz on the icy pavement, which we did. It was while we were dancing that I became aware that the band was playing the Last Waltz. How appropriate it seemed, when the lyric said, "Two lonely people together, I fell in love with you, the last waltz will last forever".

Kathleen and I at our first dance, Walsh's Super Ballroom, Listowel

Maybe it was the music, maybe it was the moon, or that Kathleen looked so beautiful, or that romance hit me in the eyes and I stammered, "Kathleen had you ever thought I might be the kind of fellow you'd like to marry?" She laughed and replied, "I have been thinking like that for some time Liam, but when we get more serious you must meet my mother".

It was during the early spring of 1963, after the snow had fully thawed, that we became close and constant companions. I was dancing one night with Kathleen, when I felt her hands roughened and wind scarred. I was surprised and gently asked her what had happened to them. She explained that her father who had done the manual work on the family farm had died five years previously and her mother, who had suffered injury to her back, had spent two years in a recovery frame in a Dublin hospital. Her only brother Denis, a member of the Garda Siochana since 1957, was stationed in the west of Ireland and therefore unable to help. The whole responsibility for the farm work had fallen on Kathleen. The only help available to her was provided by her uncle Michael, whose army training in the U.S.A. was of limited assistance in the situation.

Gortroe

Gortroe thou art a lovely spot, with lads and lasses fair
I wish to God, it were my lot, to make my dwelling there
In that lovely spot, beside the glen where the river joins in two,
And the waters bright flow down by night in the valley of Gortroe.
(Author unknown written circa 1880)

Nervous as I may have been, we both decided that the time was right to meet her mother. It was a Sunday night when Kathleen invited me to her home for tea. We had a lovely evening and we talked of many things, amongst them my own family and relations. Kathleen was sitting quite close to me, and her smile when I looked at her told me that it would be the proper time to ask her mother's permission.

Her mother smiled and said, "It is obvious that you two have made your decision for some time. Not only am I pleased, but I grant you my blessing". As the years went by, I got to know Kathleen's mother very well and can truthfully say that I found her to be one of the most decent and honourable people I ever met.

Kathleen fixed the date for our wedding, Oct. 26th 1963. On St. Patrick's Day, we went to my parents' home and broke the news to them.

Arrangements were then made for the transfer of the O'Connor family farm to Kathleen and we would reside with Kathleen's mother in the family home. It was then that I gave my notice to the Assurance Company and resigned my position as a salesman.

We had a family wedding with a few close friends who helped with the music and the singing. I was very pleased that my eldest brother, Patrick, acted as my best man and he was a wonderful Master of Ceremonies on the day. We honeymooned in Connemara and spent the last few days in Dublin before returning home. Kathleen's mother resided with us, and the three of us lived very happily and worked the farm with her mother's help and direction.

When we returned from our honeymoon and started to work the farm, Kathleen took the opportunity to show me the outline of the holding. She explained that the original farm was divided between three brothers during the famine and we would live on the part inherited by her great-Grandfather. She told me that the farm was fragmented and that I should take great care and maintain the boundaries in good condition and respect right-of-ways. People in rural Ireland believe that the land was sub-divided deliberately in this manner by the authorities, so that the land owners would disagree and, in this way, ensure that they would never unite to fight the injustices of the Landlords. There is an old saying that well maintained boundaries and fences make for good neighbours.

The farm consisted of about thirty acres. Some of the land was hilly, but the main body of the land was arable and well sheltered. There were two plots of bog, which were used for harvesting peat, the only fuel used for cooking and heating. The out offices where the cattle were wintered, the horses stabled, pigs and poultry kept, were all of stone construction and covered with wrought iron. The milking herd consisted of twelve of the most beautiful red Shorthorn cows I had ever seen. With them were two well-selected young heifer calves, which would be used for replacements. There was one horse, a pony and cart and all the horse-drawn farm machinery necessary for hay harvesting. The two-storeyed dwelling house was also stone built and covered with slate. The well-kept farmhouse and its out offices, situated on a high rise of ground, looked picturesque and blended in very well with the surrounding countryside. The dwelling house consisted of three bedrooms, parlour and kitchen-cum-living room. All the curtains and bedspreads were made by Kathleen, who, like others girls, had learned this work while attending craft classes in the village school during the long winter nights.

The Parlour or sitting room, as it was called, was the most interesting of all, as it contained a free-standing wooden cased old gramophone with a horn. Hanging on the walls were oval shaped framed photographs of Kathleen's ancestors who had emigrated to Australia or the U. S. A.

It was in these lovely surroundings that I celebrated my first Christmas away from home. In those days, Christmas night was a private time - only close friends and family visited. Of course there was no T.V. and for entertainment we played the old gramophone recordings of John McCormack and the NcNulty family, and told stories around the big open fire. The evening finished as usual with everyone joining in family prayers. I believe that Christmas in those days was celebrated with the true purpose and meaning of the occasion.

On St. Stephen's day we had our usual visit from the colourful groups of Wren boys. This was a very ancient custom, whereby the groups of girls and boys carried a bird in a cage and sang verse in each household, which ran, "The Wran, the Wran, the King of all birds, On St Stephens day he was caught in the furze, Up with the kettle and down with the pan, Please give us a few pence to bury the Wran". This custom was so widespread at the time, that one could hear the music around the countryside as they sang and played their musical instruments on their way from house to house. Following the customs of the time, Kathleen and I visited my parents' home, where a great welcome awaited us, as all the family were gathered together that same evening.

When we came back to Knocknagoshel that evening, we walked through our town-land of Gortroe and realised that we were reversing the current of young people leaving the land. So many people were leaving the area and going further a-field, that all that remained were mostly old people, and many empty houses. Kathleen explained that the old times were very tough and people had to work extremely hard just to survive. We both agreed that unless we changed our method of farming and adapted to the changing times, there'd be no future for us here either.

My first year on the farm was a learning experience, not least of which was when I sold calves on the Street market of Abbeyfeale. We had to be there at midnight in all kinds of weather and await the opening of the market. We brought our calves to town in the horse and cart. There were hundreds of farmers competing, and you had to be quick and alert to a potential sale. As the calf buyers would say mockingly when you missed an early sale when the going was good, "You have missed the first of the soup sonny boy and that is always the hottest". It was during my first night at this job that I realised I was back in farming and, whatever about the money in the Assurance business, I knew that this was the life I loved.

As the year progressed, I depended on the advice of the experienced older farmers who were my neighbours. They had told me that I would get every help from them for the first year until I had achieved a good working knowledge of this particular farm. For the cutting of the hay and the setting of the gardens, I co-operated with one of my neighbours. He had an excellent horse that we discovered would work well with mine. We worked together at the turf and general farm work. This man had a large amount of bog deal stacked on his land, which he used as firewood in his open fireplace. Today, we call this bog oak. I asked him how he had located this wood, as I knew it was buried for hundreds of years, deep in the bog.

He suggested that we both go to the bog on a frosty morning, well before sunrise, and he would show me the method he used, which had been handed down by his Grandfather. He took with him ten pointed sticks, about four feet in length, and told me to follow him. Suddenly, he stopped and said, "There is oak here" and explained that wherever there was oak underground, the frost would not have settled. Sure enough, we were looking at this spot where there was no frost at all. That's why it was essential to be there before the sun had risen and melted the general frost. The same thing applied during a snowfall. The heat from the buried wood would also have melted the snow. He continued to locate further points, and marked the ground with the rest of the sticks. Suddenly he stopped and said, "Liam do you notice something?" I replied, "No", because I did not know what he meant. He stood behind one of the markers and pointed out to me that they were all in a dead straight line. "This is the first time, I have ever come across this", he said, and with surprise on his face, he began to measure between the markers by counting his steps. When he came to the last marker, he turned to me and said "they are exactly the same distance apart and they must have been planted in this bog by some human being over a thousand years ago".

My friend had a great knowledge of nature and the wild meadows, the bogs and wildlife. Because of this background, he was able to teach me how to forecast the weather and beware of the changing climates, which were so necessary for a farmer.

We had completed our harvest in very good time and we relaxed as autumn arrived. It was during these months, that Kathleen and I decided that we would need to change our farming methods, so we sought the assistance of the local agricultural adviser, a wonderful service which was provided by the state.

Our first priority was to get running water on to the farm and into the dwelling house. We also decided to build a bathroom and kitchen on to the existing dwelling. This work was completed by early spring, and on the advice we received, we built a piggery to fatten and improve the progeny of our sow herd. To finance all these improvements, we had to mortgage our farm. We felt a little frightened at this borrowing, as it was the first time in either of our lives that we had been in debt. The piggery proved a good investment and I was able to make extra money by selling our pigs at the open market in the square at Abbeyfeale.

All was doing well and prospects were good, until disaster struck our farm in the spring of 1966. It was one morning, while working with the cattle, that I noticed something very unusual near one of my cows. All the cows seemed a bit nervous and what I discovered would send fear through any farmer, it was the dead fetus of an aborted calf. I called the veterinary surgeon immediately, who informed me that he was sure, but would know by blood tests, that this was a case of brucellosis. He advised me to bury the foetus deep in the soil and have the out offices disinfected. I was to isolate the infected animal. Similar outbreaks occurred throughout Ireland and had devastating effects for farmers generally. It also caused tremendous financial difficulties for Kathleen and myself. As our farm stock died, our milk supply dwindled and our income reduced.

Morning after morning, it was the same story, until all that was left of our milking herd, were three un-aborted cows. It was very hard on my constitution when I had to pick up the dead carcasses of calves, especially when I was advised to burn them, by pouring hot tar over them, so that no trace of the disease would remain on the ground. I worked in close contact with our veterinary surgeon, who was doing everything possible to save our herd. One morning, I told him that we had no more money to pay for his services and that we were at our wits end. He replied that it was important to restore our herd to full health and we could think of payments then. It was very unhealthy work for him also, as he sometimes worked late into the night removing decaying afterbirths from the cattle, before the disease got into the bones of the infected animal, which would result in certain death within a few days.

Late one evening, an old lady, who inquired if we had any knowledge of pishoguery, (superstition) visited us. This was enough to send a cold chill down my spine, as I heard terrible stories in my young days about people who had the power to inflict bad luck on their neighbours. She said, in a cold tone, that people who had the power to practice this evil sometimes became jealous of newly-weds, and this could be the cause of the trouble on our farm. I told a visiting priest the story as related to me by the old lady. He looked puzzled and alarmed, but made no comment about the witchcraft, and promised to bless the farm next morning. I asked the priest, as she had advised, about this superstitious practice, which was used by some people in rural Ireland who wished to bring bad luck to their neighbours. One of the best-known methods of this evil practice was to place eggs in haystacks or gardens and, as the eggs decayed, the cattle on the land pined and became unproductive, but did not die. People who possessed this evil charm were feared in the community, especially if the woman of the house was red-haired. I knew enough from my younger days not to ignore this problem, so I consulted a neighbour who was known to have a lot of knowledge about this practice. I told him that as a newcomer to the area, I felt vulnerable and even though I did not fear this superstition, I had heard enough to make me worried. He asked me to come to his house and he would tell me a true story he heard from an old Parish Clerk about this practice. He assured me that it would make my mind easy.

There was a widow woman who lived in another Parish, whose cattle had all the symptoms of being under the evil spell of pishoguery. The cattle would not thrive and looked sick, calves were born deformed and all efforts by the veterinary surgeons had failed to cure or identify this disease, or the cause of the problem. On the advice of a friend, she asked her parish priest to have the farm blessed and a Mass said in the family house. When she had fully explained to the Priest the reason why she wanted him to perform this ceremony, he asked her if she had any suspicion of who was trying to do her harm in this way. She replied that she had a good idea, but was not quite sure. The Priest promised to say the Mass as soon as possible, but warned her to invite all her neighbours and especially anyone she had suspicion of that could be involved in this pishoguery.

On the morning of the Mass, all the neighbours, including those she had suspicion of, had gathered in the kitchen awaiting the arrival of the Priest and his clerk. While the priest was putting on his vestments, the clerk was busy preparing the kitchen table, which would be used as an altar. He completed the work, by placing two brass candleholders at either side of the tabernacle on which he placed two extra long candles. During the blessing of the holy water, the priest requested the clerk to light the candles, but all efforts failed. The celebrant asked the clerk what was wrong and he replied in a shaky voice, "The blessed candles won't light, father". The priest then tried, but also failed and muttered to himself, "There is something wrong here". He addressed the congregation and in a voice just above a whisper, asked the person who was causing the trouble to leave the house, so that he could continue saying the Mass. The woman next to the door got up immediately and left the house. She was the one identified as the culprit. All eyes were turned towards the person leaving, so they did not notice the priest removing the false top from the candles. There was a strange silence in the house when the clerk lit the candles and the priest read the Mass.

Later on in the day the priest and his clerk visited the woman who had left the Mass that morning and asked for an explanation. She denied anything to do with pishoguery and said, "Father, have you anything else to do except accuse honest people of a heathen practice?" She finally disclosed what was happening only when the priest told her that he would have to report the matter to the Gardaí, for investigation. She admitted to cutting afterbirths and putting some dead animals into the water supply where her neighbours' cattle were drinking. The matter was cleaned up in a few days and my friend told me that was the last case of pishogue ever reported in that area.

Older women from the area advised me to have the farm blessed by a priest, as it looked like a case of pishogue and as a precaution, I did so. Our local priest did the blessing, saying that he thought it was a good thing to do, but told me wisely, "For goodness sake Liam, stay with your veterinary surgeon's opinion".

We survived that year without an income, mainly because we were self-sufficient in every way. We grew our own potatoes, all vegetables, had chickens, turkeys and eggs. For heat and warmth we used our own peat, which we harvested from the local bog. Luxuries were cut back on and we did not go to pictures, dances or on other outings. Being a good cook as Kathleen was, and with all the organic vegetables, we carried on regardless of being short of money. It was a difficult period in our lives, but I am pleased to say that we benefitted greatly from learning to survive and, in retrospect, our understanding of, and respect for each other grew.

By the following spring our luck had changed as the cattle had recovered, our milk was increasing and our new-born calves were healthy and strong. At this stage, we aimed to increase the income from our farm, so we called on the advice of an agricultural adviser. Part of the plan was to supply the farmyard with running water, to increase our sow herd and to fatten their progeny to suitable weight for purchase by the factory. With a bank loan, we completed our piggery unit and had piped water installed throughout the entire farm by the end of that year. We built a kitchen and became the proud owners of the first bathroom and toilet in this area. With the advantage of the running water, we were able to install a milking machine, which, of course, brought great ease, compared to the time consuming and laborious hand milking. It was at this time that I regretfully sold my horse and pony and the old horse machinery and invested in a second-hand Ferguson twenty diesel tractor and the necessary farm machinery. We had regained our confidence and the future was looking bright. We knew there was hard work ahead, but the rewards would be worth it.

Dancing was back for us and we resumed going to the pictures and if we were not harvesting hay on Sundays, we would make our way to the seaside. Early in spring, just a little after dawn, I would round up my milking herd and drive them to the farmyard, where Kathleen would be waiting to help me with the milking. I loved this time of day as I walked along listening to the singing of birds and the chatter of wild life as they announced, in their own way, the start of a new day. I also loved to observe the beauty of the countryside and watch the mists lifting and evaporating in the morning sunshine. This was a great time to observe the antics of the birds and animals and listen to the sounds coming from the nearby stream, as it would give a good indication of weather conditions to come. If the crows in the nearby rookery started squawking in a loud chatter and then settled quietly in the trees, or if there was an unusual loud sound coming from the river, this indicated rain was not too far away. However if the crane was fishing up stream and the swallows were flying high you could be sure of a long period of fine weather.

Darkness

Mise Raifteirí an file lán dochas is grá
Le súile gan solas, le ciúnas gan crá,
Ag dul siar ar m'aistear le solas mo chroí,
Fann agus tuirseach go deireadh mo shlí;
(Raifteirí)

(English Translation)
I am Raftery, the poet full of hope and love
With eyes without light, in silence without
torment,
Going back on my journey with the light of
my heart,
Drifting and tired to the end of my days.

One morning, while observing the sunrise on the distant hills, I was surprised to see it surrounded by a halo of blue haze. I dismissed it as an unusual occurrence, but to my surprise, it reappeared morning after morning. If the morning was foggy I found it difficult to locate the cows in the field. I overcame this difficulty by driving the cattle grazing near the gate on to the roadway and, sure enough, as soon as the other cattle missed them, they would come rushing to join the main herd.

In the following weeks and months I began to notice that there was very little twilight and that darkness came down rather suddenly. When working with neighbours, I would be requested to locate a farm implement which would be standing a few yards away. When I could not find it immediately, I would hear the men say, "It is time to wake up Liam, you'll walk into it if you're not careful". One evening, when returning late from visiting a neighbour, I walked straight into a cattle truck which was parked near to the entrance to my home. The impact left me stunned for a while, but as there was no physical damage done, I did not tell my wife Kathleen of the incident. I was now avoiding doing any work with farm machinery and if I had to drive by car to town, I would make sure to return by early afternoon. Selling cattle in the early morning darkness was always very difficult for me, as I would not be able to recognise the dealer who was buying my cattle. This was very important to the seller, as you had to keep a keen eye on his facial expressions and movements, so you would know when to sell at the highest price possible. I now realized that I was only responding to the greetings of people by the sound of their voices. I tried to avoid any thoughts or worry about this problem, as I had read about an eye condition which caused a problem between daylight and darkness. The term to describe this condition was night-blindness. I was happy with this conclusion and decided all that was necessary for me to lead a normal life, was to adjust my lifestyle to suit the occasion.

One morning, before returning home from the fair, I went with a friend to a bar for refreshments. I was surprised to hear my name being discussed by two men who had their backs turned to me. One of the men said, "I met Liam Lynch on the street this morning and he just walked past without saying hello, did you hear he was left a substantial legacy or won a lot of money in a lottery? His attitude gives the impression that he is getting too big for his boots". The other man replied in a quiet tone, "I will talk to you later, you'd never know what might be troubling that poor man". On my way home from the fair that morning, I was suddenly overcome with a great sense of lone-liness and shame at what I had heard. Within a short distance of home, I had regained my composure. There and then I vowed that whatever problem I had with my eyes, I would do everything in my power to overcome it.

With harvesting completed in good time, Kathleen and I decided we would attend the Rose Festival in Tralee for an evening's entertainment. At the outskirts of Tralee, Kathleen became concerned about my driving. She was worried that I didn't appear to have seen a pedestrian in dark clothing who was walking near the car. I thought nothing of it and at first blamed it on the bad lights of the Volkswagen. Kathleen said that I should go and have my sight tested, which I did shortly afterwards.

When the optician had completed his tests, he prescribed glasses, but explained that they would be only of limited help. I returned to my farm work with renewed confidence, but had to dispose of them in a few months, as they became more of a hindrance than help. As time passed, my sight deteriorated and I was getting very worried.

On a doctor's advice, I decided to consult an eye specialist in Dublin. I had a thorough examination and when I asked the consultant for his diagnosis, he asked if any of my family were with me as he would like to talk to them. He spoke to my brother in private, before telling me that I would get a letter outlining the diagnosis and prognosis in a week or so.

I was anxiously awaiting the postman and I will never forget the place and time I received the results. I was drawing hay on my twenty-diesel tractor when the postman stopped me and handed me a letter which contained the consultant's report. I was able to read the diagnosis and was shocked and alarmed at the results. I had a degenerative condition of the eye with the medical term, Retinitis Pigmentosa or R. P. for short. The best I could hope for was that I would retain some limited vision, but the likelihood in my case, was that I would go blind. I read the report again and again, and decided that I would not show it to my wife Kathleen until I had time to reflect on it.

I looked around and suddenly the hills of Knocknagoshel became the loveliest and most beautiful in the world. I had a little place, which I called my own, on the banks of the river which flowed through our farm. It could only be entered by a gap in the furze bushes and when you sat there for while, all troubles seemed to vanish. Here, on a fine day, I would sit for hours watching the trout playing in the pools and sometimes I would throw a pebble in their direction, just to watch them jump to the shadows for protection. I was so nostalgic that I went to this spot by the river and cried my sadness. On the following day, I completed the drawing home of the hay, but for some reason, did not put the last cock in the barn. I was in deep thought, wondering how I would break the news of the doctor's report to Kathleen.

I was looking for a place of solitude, so I went to the piggery, which was located about two hundred yards from our dwelling house. I was standing with my elbows on the wall, drained of all emotion and desperately trying to get my thoughts together. I was unaware of somebody standing close to me, until I heard Kathleen say in a calm voice, "Liam, what is it that makes you weep so much?" I handed her the letter without turning and waited for what seemed like eternity for her reply. Finally, she spoke, saying, "All is not lost yet, Liam. I have read that they have made great progress in other countries treating serious eye problems and in some cases even successfully restored sight". On our way home, she said, "They have also successfully transplanted eyes. I am sure you know, Liam, you will be welcome to one of mine". With these kind reassuring words and the placing of her hands on my shoulder, I felt much better and my confidence was restored.

As my sight deteriorated, I had no choice but to stop driving the car. Kathleen took over this responsibility and for some time drove the tractor and learned to operate the farm machinery. Most of the heavy farm work, such as milking the cows, harvesting the peat removing the main agricultural crops from the fields, I was just capable of at this stage. In the cool of the evening, I usually ended my day's work tending and admiring my kitchen garden. One evening, I was joined in my garden by a neighbour for a chat. He was a frequent visitor and a good friend. I was talking directly to him in the changing light, when I noticed, to my horror, that all I could see clearly was the movement on one side of his face.

That disturbing scene stayed in my mind and signalled the beginning of a period of terrible trauma in my life.

Shortly afterwards, I started having unusual nightmares. I would be playing a game in brilliant sunshine with my friends. Suddenly, there would be nothing but empty darkness. I would awaken with a start, and it would take me some time to realise that I was only dreaming, but by then I would be frightened and perspiring profusely. The dreams became more intense in their frequency, but the vision kept changing from time to time. Sometimes, there would be a group of about ten crows or so standing very quietly on an old timber gate. Slowly, they would grow darker in colour, until all that would be visible were their shiny black eyes. Suddenly, they would open their beaks as if to call, but there would be no sound. All that would remain to be seen was the red colour of their mouths and throats.

In the evening as darkness approached, I began to fear, more and more, what the night dreaming held in store for me. Sometimes, the dreaming seemed to fade for a while and I got a few weeks of peaceful sleep at night, without interruption. When the dreaming resumed, it usually became more frequent and intense. In this nightmare, I would be standing on a fence, checking and counting our cattle to make sure they were all present and secure. The herd would start to slowly fade and the fence would crumble from under my feet. A dark tunnel would then open and I would fall helplessly down and down into this dark hole, for what seemed like an eternity. When I awakened and became aware of my surroundings, I would switch on the light in the bathroom to make sure it was there, before washing the sweat from my body. Before morning, the same dream would resume, but in this turbulent vision, my head would be hitting off the side of the tunnel as I somersaulted into that endless black hole.

After this nightmare, I was lying awake in a confused state for some time. In this state of mind, I put my hand on my face for reassurance that I had not suffered any cuts or bruising during the fall.

However, I felt a soft sticky substance, which I felt almost certain was blood. Before going to the bathroom, I again put my hand to my forehead, placed my fingers in my mouth to indicate if the sticky substance tasted of blood. It had that same salty taste of blood, so I carefully washed and dried my face, placing the towel where Kathleen would see it. She would surely recognise any traces of blood on it in the daylight. By now I was quite awake and realised that the substance on my forehead was heavy sweat, caused by that horrible nightmare. These dreams were very intense and I became more worried when they started to interfere with my daily work.

I became more introverted and withdrawn and, for the first time, I felt that I was not discussing this problem openly with Kathleen. I avoided all contact as much as possible with the outside world and began to live more and more within my own territory. I stopped going to films, which I loved, and stopped going to football matches with my friends because these occasions would cause me embarrassment as I would not be able to give an opinion. I had loved visiting my old home on a regular basis, but this, after some time, became more of a torment than a joy. It was here, in the fields where I grew up, that the real extent of my visual impairment became more evident to me. I could make my way along the road but I could not clearly make out the fields and houses of my friends and neighbours. All that could be seen in this area was in my mind's eye.

Secretly, I started to make novenas and prayed that some healing power would come upon my eyes. This was not happening, so the greatest fear in my mind started to develop - not alone that I would lose my sight but that I would lose my identity in the community. I thought that the only future I had was that I would be seated in a dark room listening to a radio forever.

Mental Healing

"I am not a mechanism, an assembly of various sections.
And it is not because the mechanism is working wrongly,
that I am ill, I am ill because of wounds to the soul, to the deep emotional self..."

(D.H. Lawrence)

It was then that my friends, who I'm sure were in contact with Kathleen, asked me if I would like to go on a pilgrimage to Lourdes. At first I declined the offer, but as I had never been outside the country on a holiday, something within my mind told me that I should go. In August 1971, accompanied by my father and my aunt, a presentation convent nun, Therese, we started on our journey to Lourdes. We stayed in Dublin the night before in a small hotel, and in the morning I made my own way to the dining room. I could hear all the early breakfast-goers talking, but was completely unaware that there were five steps leading down to the dining area. I was walking quite briskly when suddenly I felt my feet go. I avoided serious injury by quickly grabbing hold of a railing, preventing me from falling down the steps.

I was seated next to a young man on the plane, and after a while it became quite obvious to me that he was a priest. He asked me if I was accompanying my father to Lourdes, and I replied, "No, that it was he that was helping me." "What is your problem?" he enquired "and why so are you on this pilgrimage?" I explained to him that I had an eye condition that would lead to permanent blindness. He said then in a quiet tone, "I hope you're not expecting to be cured there." I replied in a similar tone, "What do you think is taking me there?" "There are very few cures at Lourdes", he said, but I replied, "The first miracle there was a cure for blindness, do you not remember the blind man seated on the ground and the water flowing under him. He just wet his hands and rubbed them to his eyes and he was cured immediately". "If I were you", he said, "I would pray for peace of mind". "That is fine", I replied, "I will have plenty of peace of mind if I get my sight back". "If you have true faith", he said, "everything is possible, do you remember that quotation?" "Good on you", I replied, "you have thrown the ball into my court now and it will be my own fault if I am not cured". Suddenly he got up to talk to the other passengers on the plane and did not return.

When I arrived in Lourdes, I went on a midnight visit to the Grotto. Here, for the first time, I met people who had far more serious problems than me. There were no other blind people present, just others suffering from mental illness, weeping sores and many other complaints too many to mention. We all started to meditate and then prayed together. Suddenly I found myself praying for others and forgetting my own problem. I continued my pilgrimage visiting the Grotto, usually at midnight, meeting these people and praying with them. Slowly but surely, I was becoming aware of how lucky I was compared to others. I believe part of the power of prayer is that it has a self-hypnotic effect on one's own mind. I don't know what the visit to Lourdes did for me, but something happened there that gave me a great purpose and resolve to face the future. I started to enjoy it and, believe it or not, it ended for me as a wonderful holiday. I was also glad to be there with my father, because for the first time since I married, we shared each other's thoughts and company. It was the first time I discussed openly, the seriousness of my eye condition with him. I enquired of him how long he had been aware of my problem. He said he had known only since the eye specialist in Listowel had asked him to visit his clinic to discuss my problem. He continued with great emotion, "We both know, Liam, so would you mind if we leave it at that?" I was probably glad to end the discussion at the time and we never again spoke of the problem. He then said, "I am seventy two years of age, but I could still assist you on the farm, or with the buying or selling of cattle in the mart". He came to work with me on the bog after that, but it was obvious that he would not be able to continue with this sort of work for much longer.

It was in the spring of '79 that I got a call from Listowel to say that my father was seriously ill and that death was near. To my great sadness, I did not get there in time, but was very comforted when I heard that my mother, sister, and brothers, were with him in his final hours. Mass was arranged and the funeral took place in our parish church, Ballydonoghue, a few days later. My brothers and I shouldered the coffin and placed it in the hearse. As I was not capable of driving, I was given the honour of sitting in the front seat of the hearse, to accompany my father's remains on the final journey to Lislaughtin Abbey. As the cortege moved slowly away, many old memories came to haunt my mind, such as the donkeys following us to Mass. We passed the old Blackwood cross and straight by my father's farmland at a very slow pace. We stopped briefly at the gate outside our family home; here my mind went blank for some time. As we laid him to rest by the old Abbey wall that he loved so well, I could almost hear his voice, as he said to me many years ago, "Never forget your grandfather, and always pray for his soul". As I moved away from the grave, my mind was full of emotion and I found it very hard to come to any understanding of my own personal thoughts. Then I remembered some verses from Paddy Kavanagh's poem, "In memory of my father", and I repeated it over and over to myself. I have never forgotten those lines and to this day, I find them a great consolation:

Every old man I see
Reminds me of my father
When he had fallen in love with death
One time when sheaves were gathered

Every old man I see
In October coloured weather
Seems to say to me
I was once your father.

(Patrick Kavanagh)

On returning home, I continued to help Kathleen to run the farm. At this point, even though I was not driving the car, I was still driving the tractor in the fields. I was still capable of manual work and with the help of a neighbour, set my vegetable garden and sowed my potatoes in *taobhfhóds*. I continued to keep a herd of sows to help generate extra income. This was difficult work and, as one of my friends used to say, "Liam, will you be up again tonight doing matron to a sow?" It is true that I would be up all night watching bonhams being farrowed, to make sure that they would not be smothered in the process. In my lifetime I have often heard the term, "He is as ignorant as a pig". This statement is ignorant in itself, for

I was often there to witness the great care and intuitive love the sow took of her progeny. I would stand well out of the way as she made her bed of straw and as each bonham was farrowed, they would go to her head and chat with her. She would stretch out and make room for them to attach to the little teats. The smallest one, usually called the íochtar, would always make its way to the mother's head. He would chat eagerly to her, before retiring to the furthest away teat where milk would flow and he would suck vigorously and eventually end up falling asleep contentedly. How she accomplished this always amazed me. By morning, she usually had twelve in her family, and for the next six to eight weeks she looked after this family completely on her own. Some feat for what we humans call a stupid and ignorant animal.

I know too from experience, that sows sometimes suffer great emotional distress following the farrowing of a litter. If you were not present at this particular time, they might kill and eat their own progeny. Experience will teach a person to be very careful at this time, because a sow can attack and seriously injure a person. The local cure for this, was to go to the nearby pub and get the slop or waste stout from the night before and give it to the animal to drink. I have seen sows drink this stout with great relish and, I suppose, this is where the term "He could drink like a pig", derives from. About a quarter of an hour after drinking the stout, the sow would fall into a deep sleep. When she awoke, there would be no further occurrence of this emotional distress.

In the early eighties, I found that my income from the farm had dwindled and we found it hard to keep up with the day to day payments. The government's decision to remove the non-mean tested farmers' dole, contributed greatly to this difficulty. I believed at the time, that the removal of this small income would do untold damage to small farm families in the disadvantaged areas. Through the local I.C.M.S.A. (Irish Creamery Milk Suppliers Association) branch, I started a campaign to oppose this ridiculous decision. All politicians were asked to come to a meeting in the community centre in Knocknagoshel to answer questions and give their views on this issue. The newspapers also covered this campaign, and most people in rural Ireland agreed that the decision to remove this payment was very wrong. However, the letters to the editors, and the Gay Byrne radio show in particular, gave the opposite view. These intellectual writers to the papers and to the Gay Byrne programme, some of whom I believe must have had their roots in the country, supported the government of the day. The voice of the ordinary people in the country failed to match these intellectual contributors and, in 1983, to the horror of all the people living in disadvantaged areas, the scheme was abandoned. The politicians, who had promised us so much, did absolutely nothing and were only using the issue to promote themselves. The farming organisation of which I was a member at the time did not sufficiently support our cause. However, when these same organisations were petitioning the government on another issue, or for more money at budget time, they were never slow to use the decline of the small farmers in Ireland as a bargaining point. In reference to this decision, one man said to me laughingly, "Remember, Liam, that it is always the big cow at the silage pit that gets the most". A friend advised me at that time, that due to my circumstances, I should apply for a means tested blind pension. I had my sight tested once again and sent in my application to the Department of Social Welfare. I felt very bad about this, because it was a further step in drawing my attention to the fact that I would be blind and unable to earn my own income. I discussed this matter with Kathleen, who understood my anxiety, but who also knew that we had no other choice.

Sometime later, I was working in my garden, when I heard a car driving up towards my house. The driver got out of his car and, seeing me working, asked if I was a resident of this house. He had a briefcase in his hand and said he was looking for a William Lynch of Gortroe, Knocknagoshel. I politely said that I was that that person. "No", he replied, "it's a much older person I am looking for. Is your father or uncle about?" I explained that my father was dead and that I was the man he was looking for. He said, "Sir, I have very little time to waste and the man I am looking for is much older and has applied for the old age pension".

I replied with a smile, "I have a T.D. who promised me during the last election that, if I voted for him, he would get me the pension.". "I have no time to be wasting on the likes of you", he said quickly and turned in the direction of his car. "Have you seen the full contents of that application, sir?" I called out. "Please examine them carefully". Attached to the application was, of course, my eye report. Having examined the papers, he looked in my direction sympathetically and said, "Are you really this man?" When I answered, he asked me if I would accompany him to my kitchen where we could discuss the subject further. There was a lot of talk in the country of how unreasonable and cold these pension officers were. Before examining the papers, that man asked every question about my sight in a very caring manner and, asked me how I saw the future. He turned to Kathleen, who was standing by and said, "I am very sorry ma'm, to see you two people in this predicament and hope that I can do something positive to help you". He asked Kathleen if we could sell off the farm animals. She replied that she would like to and showed her blackened hand, which had been kicked by a cow that morning during milking.

He told me that he would grant me half the pension and half that again to Kathleen and that this would amount to forty-five pounds a week. On departing, he said that he would check the file again the following day, and to our surprise and delight we were granted an extra five pounds a week. Therefore, at the age of forty-three years of age, I was granted the old age pension, the only pension available to blind people at the time.

In and around the middle eighties, there was a renewed influx of tourists returning to find their roots from all corners of the world. They would only be here for a short time, when they would ask to see the house where their ancestors were born. One of these visitors was a young Australian law student, Peter Gray, whose grandmother was born in our old farmhouse in Gortroe.

Peter Gray's Homecoming

"Home is the place where, when you have to go there,
They have to take you in"

(Robert Frost)

I remember well the day he came to the door and asked if it would be alright if he stayed for a night or two. Kathleen said that of course we would be delighted to have him, for as long as he wished. She cooked him a lovely meal, which he thoroughly enjoyed, and we chatted for hours before going to bed. Some of the neighbours called in to welcome Peter and the pleasure could be seen on his face when an older man remembered the morning his grand-mother left for Australia, never again to return.

He started working with me the following morning on the farm and, as they say, he took to it as if he had been born into it. He had a great love of animals and in return, they took immediately to his gentle nature. The following evening, I asked him at about ten o'clock, if he would like to go for a pint of stout to the local village. He thought that it was a little late to be

Peter, Liam and "Pandit" the dog, heading to work on the farm

going out and that, if we did go, he would like Kathleen to come. "She is ready to go", I said. At ten thirty or thereabouts, we entered Neil Con Connie's Pub, where some of my friends were already engaged in drinking creamy pints of Guinness. When Peter was introduced to them, he was informed that it was the true test of a man to see if he could drink and hold a gallon of stout or more. He drank his first pint and declared that he was capable of being initiated as a true Knocknagoshel man. The music and singing started later and the local policeman, who was well able to drink, joined us. He informed us that we could stay until morning as there was no fear of the patrol car coming. The music continued and after a good few pints and with Kathleen's help, Peter started to dance the polka sets and seemed to be thoroughly enjoying himself. I can well remember him at four o'clock in the morning singing "Carrickfergus" and boasting that he had just drunk a gallon of stout.

Peter had a great understanding of my visual impairment and was a great help assisting me around the farm. We continued to work together and I found his eagerness to learn about his roots to be very interesting. He evidently enjoyed working on the farm because he returned again and again. He was amazed at the amount of co-operation between the neighbours, especially when he heard that all the locals had set their gardens in one neighbour's field. This included the local Garda, who came and not only set his own, but would help if you had not completed yours. One day, Peter and I spent a day in the bog cutting turf with a neighbour. Peter must have been the talk of the place, when people heard that he had presented said neighbour with a bottle of whiskey in gratitude for the pleasure of working in his bog. On our way home across the fields that evening, I remarked to Peter, that if I were to go blind, then Gortroe was the best place in the world for it to happen, the reason being that the neighbours were so helpful and caring. By the late eighties, Peter had reluctantly returned to Australia to set up his law practice.

By the mid eighties, modernisation and change in farming attitudes had begun to make life easier. Contract silage-making had done away with the laborious work of hay saving. By this stage, all of my neighbours had tractors and formed themselves into a "meitheal".

This meant that one of them would collect my milk daily, which spared me the difficult task of delivering it to the creamery. By this time, I had started using a bamboo cane to help me get around and it was quite successful. This was the era when every organization and Co-op in the country held their annual dinner dance in the hotels. I attended most of these events, but my favourite outing was the

"A man is nearer to God's heart in a garden than anywhere else on earth." My loyal and trusted friend, Patrick Phil O Connor, Gortroe, Knocknagoshel

Fealesbridge, Headley's Bridge Creamery Social. I began to really enjoy outings with my friends and a dance with Kathleen was always on the cards. I must say I improved at the dancing and was often asked for a dance by my neighbours' wives. Life seemed to be blooming again for Kathleen and myself.

On the 29th of June, 1987, our house was filled with great sadness at the death of Kathleen's mother, my mother in-law, Nell C. O'Connor. She was a great person and a wonderful help to both of us in running the farm, and in our daily lives. I remember well when times were bad, she would always say, "God is good, tomorrow will be better". Very often she was right.

It was a beautiful summer, weather-wise, and there was an abundant harvest, as well as lots of peat for the following year. By early August we had plenty on our hands, so we decided that on some Sundays, we would go for a drive around different parts of Kerry. Kathleen would get a packed lunch and we would drive to one of the scenic places, like Caragh Lake or to the seaside. On one occasion, we took a trip up to the west of Ireland. The neighbours were wonderful in coming every day to take care of the cattle while we were away.

This was our first real holiday since we got married and we both enjoyed it thoroughly. Kathleen would describe to me the things I could not see clearly. I thank God that Kathleen was able to describe those wonderful scenes; they are still very vivid in my mind. It was as we crossed the Gap of Maamore in Co. Donegal and headed out for Malin Head, that we discussed the prospect of selling our cows. We were enjoying the holiday and the freedom and this probably helped us to make this painful decision. On returning home, we contacted the cattle mart at Castleisland and, after inspecting our herd, the manager said that the eighth of December would be a good day to have a sale. He also told us to leave all the arrangements in his hands and not to worry about anything. Many farmers in the Knocknagoshel area were doing likewise for various reasons and sadly, by the year 2000, all that remained of the original thirteen dairy farming families in the Gortroe townland, was one. Having worked for the greater part of my life with these people, I felt very sad that this way of life had come to an end.

End of an Era - Stable Echoes

By eerie sounds of silence through led. Last
milking frozen, commemorated by chains
extended to their nails,
Milk pails dusty fusting rusting red,
Manger splendid that would never more be
nurture mended,
Forlorn deserted dereliction of an outhouse
by a homestead extended.

                    (John Malachy Raftery, Galway)

We were awakened at 7a.m on Thursday the 8th Of December, by the sound of a lorry approaching our house. It reversed to the stall door and we drove half our dairy herd into the truck. These were very quiet animals and some of them looked very nervous as they walked up the ramp. Kathleen and I spoke of anything and everything, except the selling of the cows. The quietness and silence around the yard and house that morning was palpable. Some time later the lorry returned again and the remainder of our herd was driven onto the truck, the door closed, and they were driven away. Farming life, as Kathleen and I knew it had come to an end.

Later in the afternoon, we drove to the mart and witnessed the farmers appraising our herd, consulting, talking and evaluating. The manager opened the sale and told the farmers that this was a great opportunity to buy a replacement for their herds. There was a brisk demand and the cattle were sold off quickly. Finally, I heard the manager saying, "This is the last cow in the herd and surely the finest in the bunch". I took one look at her and was surprised to see that she was the cow that was a descendant of the Samaritan that my father and mother had given to Kathleen and myself as a wedding present The buying for this cow started and it was clear that she was in great demand. I turned and walked away quickly. I knew the price rising by the increasingly rapid tones of the auctioneer. I never heard her final price; I just did not want to know.

As time went by, I often visited the cow house and there is something sad and lonely about the quietness of an empty stall. I was finding it very difficult to pass the time and started doing messages and shopping for my neighbours on shank's mare. Christmas came and we were delighted when Kathleen's brother and his wife and family joined us for the festive season. It was during this period that I got a very interesting package from the National Council for the Blind in Cork. It was a cassette book, by Walter Macken, called "The Bog Man". I sat and listened to the first cassette and was enthralled by his account of life on a farm in rural Ireland. I have read this book over and over again and every time I read it, I seem to get more enjoyment from it. The description in this book of life in rural Ireland was exactly as I had known it. The taped books proved to be a wonderful asset to my life, as I could pass hours and hours sitting by my fireside on a rainy day listening to them, and as a result, I became an avid reader.

Spring had come, when we got a letter from our cousin Peter Gray in Australia. He had become very successful in his profession as a solicitor and had been part of a team that had just won a difficult case in the High Court in Sidney. The letter contained an invitation to Kathleen and myself to join him for a prolonged holiday at his home in Sydney the following September. Kathleen, though terrified of flying, in her excitement said, "It is too good an offer not to accept". We actually danced with excitement at the prospect and wrote immediately accepting his generous offer. Soon after, tickets for our trip arrived in the post. Little else was talked about during that summer, except our upcoming holiday. Then came the great day, and Kathleen's brother and wife saw us off at Shannon Airport. At this stage, Peter also announced that he would be getting married during our visit. As a wedding gift, we took a Waterford crystal wedding-knife to be used to cut the wedding cake.

Security was very strict at London Airport and an explanation was demanded of us as to what use we had for the knife. Kathleen told them what it was for and the man behind the desk, smilingly asked where the cake was. She opened her luggage bag and showed him the cake she had baked for Peter's wedding. He again smiled and said we would get the knife back on arrival in Sydney and wished us a happy holiday. This happy incident made us feel very much at ease and the rest of our journey to Australia passed comfortably. We stopped at Bangkok and I was totally amazed at the amount of small people who insisted on calling me sir and persisted in trying to sell me jewellery. Kathleen was laughing heartily when she heard me trying to tell them that I didn't want any, but they persisted, and eventually I bought a little brooch for Kathleen.

When we arrived at Kingsway Smith Airport, the plane crew had informed the staff of my eye problem. We were treated like royalty, and later I was to discover that people with disabilities were treated with great respect in Australia, much as wounded war veterans. As I stepped on Australian soil, I felt very proud, as I was the fourth generation of the Lynch family to have arrived there. I had had relatives there to the best of my knowledge, as all my uncles and granduncles were Catholic clergymen. We were very warmly greeted by Peter, who was absolutely delighted to see us. He took us to his residence at King's Cross, where we had a long rest until the following morning. For the first few days, Peter showed us around Sydney, and then told us we were on our own. After this, we went exploring the City's museums and its beautiful parks, so filled with the strange sounds of unusual wild life. On our way home one evening, Kathleen said jokingly to me, "Do you remember a place called Knocknagoshel?" We were enjoying our holiday so much that we had forgotten about home. We saw what for us was a strange sight on our way home that evening. Girls dressed in the flimsiest of clothing, chatting with men and after discussions, going away with them in their cars. A man with a ponytail, who told us that there was a strip show starting shortly in his premises, accosted us. It would cost us thirty dollars to go. We refused and went on our way. While Kathleen went to a shop nearby, one of the girls made me a proposition for the night. I was tickled to death at this, but was very glad when Kathleen rejoined me and we made our way home.

As we walked along, I explained to Kathleen that I was ashamed that the girl propositioned me. How she laughed until the tears streamed down her face, when she said that the girl wouldn't have asked unless you looked like a likely client. Our room was located at the top of a four-story building and in order to gain access to it, we had to have a key to open a steel gate. On one occasion, I had forgotten the key to the main entrance and I had to call a person on the intercom to open the door from the inside. Having given our full details, we were finally admitted by a girl who had her head shaven: one of the Hare Krishnas. She advised us, politely, to always carry the keys to the premises in a remote part of our clothing. She said that some of the people living in the building would not like to be interrupted late at night. She was very mannerly and this was a surprise to me as she looked very strange with her shaved head and kimono. I was expecting something different for I had seldom encountered people outside my own religion or way of life. Our room was very well equipped with modern conveniences and Kathleen did all the cooking and also made her own bread. Part of my work was to brush the room onto the landing and down to the next floor. I was working away at my job and was unaware that there was a person standing by until she spoke. It was the girl that had admitted us the night before. She seemed anxious to talk so we both sat down on the stairs.

She told me of her way of life and the reason she was a member of this sect. I was very impressed. It seemed she had given up on her material life and had devoted herself to helping the underprivileged. She was very interested in the stories I had to tell her from Ireland, especially as I was the first Irishman she had had a real conversation with. I told her stories from my youth and how Ireland had gained her independence from Britain. We discussed my religion, Catholicism, and found that very little separated us in our basic beliefs. I must have been talking to her for an hour when Kathleen called me and said that I had been up to my old tricks again!

Later on in the day, down in St. Martin's Place, there was a musical Hare Krishna procession. We were standing admiring them when my new friend raised her hand from among them and said "How are you enjoying life Liam?" We were enjoying our stay in Australia, more so when we were invited by a friend to the horseracing track in Sydney. We would have to dress in suits as we were going to be in the owners and trainers corporate box. I was awaiting a taxi outside our lodgings when a man said to me, "Hello, how are you?" I was surprised at this but replied and asked him did he think the day would hold up - keep fine. "I thought by the look of you, you were Irish, and now that you've mentioned the weather I'm dead sure".

His name was Tom O'Shaughnessy and he told me that his Grandfather had immigrated to Australia from somewhere in Cork. I did not place any bet during the races as I was not used to the going. Then I noticed a horse was running, ridden by a jockey named Mickey Lynch. I placed a whopper of a bet on him and to my surprise, and to the surprise of all the punters present, he won by a short head. How the owners and trainers joked, "You must be a very wealthy man Liam, not only are you out on holidays here but you also have your own personal jockey!"

We were enjoying our holiday and getting quite used to the city's buses and trains. We visited many of the great museums, zoos and parks and went by ferry across Sydney Bay to Doyles on the Waterfront for their famous fish and chips. One Sunday evening, we were walking down along Circular Quay when I heard a piper playing the traditional Irish and Scottish tunes. I spoke to him and told him I was out from Ireland. He just smiled but, when I was a hundred yards down the street, I heard the familiar sound of Molly Malone echoing after me. There was a great carnival atmosphere and great entertainment in this area and there were acts from many parts of the world. There was a huge ring and this artist was asking people to come and take part in his show. Very few volunteered, and I was greatly surprised when my own Kathleen and a Japanese girl joined him. When he spoke to the Japanese girl he said jestingly, "Do you own half of Sydney?"

When Kathleen announced that she was Irish, he spoke very slowly and sarcastically to her saying, "Will you be able to understand what I am saying?" Kathleen smiled and replied "I think so". The show involved the man transferring money from hand to hand with the speed of a three-card-trick man. Try as he could, he could never outfox Kathleen. The audience kept on applauding until, finally, he became frustrated and asked Kathleen to go away. There were some Americans of Irish descent in the audience, and they each congratulated her and said she did herself and Ireland proud. As we continued on our way, we inquired at a tourist office for the whereabouts of an Irish pub. A woman gave us very clear and detailed directions but, as she finished, she smiled and said "Ye'll hear it before ye see it".

She was correct, and from a good distance away we could hear the familiar sounds of traditional Irish music and singing. As we sat in the pub that evening, we never felt more at home since we went on our holiday. The only thing that seemed out of place to me, was the big black woman behind the counter filling the pints of Guinness. There were people there from all over Ireland, and when they heard that we were out on holiday, we didn't have to buy a drink. As it was coming to the close of our holiday, we stayed on late into the evening with our many new friends and had to get a taxi home for the first time while we were out there.

On the following day, we made a final tour of this lovely city and when we boarded a bus to visit the City Aquarium, Kathleen said, "Do you know Liam, we're becoming like city folk". The last part of the journey to the Aquarium we had to walk, and we went slightly astray. Kathleen said she was a good judge of character and could always pick out a decent person to ask when we were lost. We asked this woman if she could give directions but she replied that she wasn't quite sure, "You see I'm from the country myself!"

We said our goodbye to our newly married good friend and host, Peter Gray, soon after at Kingsway Smith Airport. There were tears in his eyes as he said goodbye and asked us to promise to return.

On our way home via Hawaii, we saw the sun rise and set within two hours. The plane journey was very entertaining and I asked one of the stewards if the pilot would allow me to join him in the cockpit. She requested my passport and within twenty minutes returned smiling and replied that yes, the captain would like to see you. He was a very nice man and as I entered the cockpit, he started with a few words of Danny Boy. On his instructions I sat on a seat and he allowed me, under strict supervision, to experience what it was like to be a pilot, explaining how the radio and landing gear operated, the altitude the plane was flying and the reasons for it. Having completed his demonstration, he jokingly said, "I suppose Liam you think you've done everything now?" I replied with a smile and said, "Yes, but I've also done something you've never done". "What's that he enquired?" How he laughed when I told him that I had driven a donkey and cart with milk to the creamery in Ballylongford. "I'm sure I know what you mean", he said, "and I'm pretty sure that I will never have that experience".

Coming at a time when my eyesight was finally deteriorating, I believe that it was very important to have seen how people live on the other side of the world. I will never forget my trip to Australia and sometimes at night when I lie awake I can switch on my mind's video and relive every moment with great enjoyment. I think that having lost my sight I can recall very clearly great moments in my sighted life.

We arrived in New York in late autumn to spend the last few days of our journey with Kathleen's cousins. We journeyed upstate to their residence in the Catskill Mountains along the Hudson River. This part of the world really looks beautiful at this time of year. The mountains and little streams blended in beautifully with the golden colours on the trees, and I'll never forget the feeling when I passed a little bridge named after Rip Van Winkle, which brought back memories of when I first read this story as a young boy. We were greeted warmly by Kathleen's Uncle, who had immigrated to the United States in the 1920s. We talked long into the night and, by morning, I don't think that there was a neighbour in Knocknagoshel he hadn't enquired about. His burning love for Ireland, but especially for his old townland of Gortroe, was ever present. He would never visit Ireland again as he had an incapacitating disease. We visited some of the nicest and most scenic areas around Carmel, the county town of Puttnam County. It was here that I took my final picture with a camera. It was a statue of that 16-year-old heroine, Sybil Ludington, astride the great stallion Star. It was she that rode through all the New England states on this horse, to warn the peasants that the redcoats were approaching. I believe that this girl's heroism was equal to that of Paul Revere.

We arrived back in Ireland just in time for the onset of winter. It was difficult to get back into the routine of normal life. This was not helped by my becoming redundant as a farmer. I was still capable of helping my neighbours with difficult calving births and was often called in the middle of the night to assist. I also started to walk a lot and was able to do so without the assistance of a white cane. However, out of my own area I was like a fish out of water, and would always have to have the assistance of Kathleen or a friend. I was advised by the social worker to go for mobility training but I said that I could never do so while my mother was alive.

For some strange reason I believed that it would kill her to see me blind and using a cane. Little did I know that she was the one person who was imploring my family to get me to do mobility training. They only told me this when she died. My mother was almost 96 when she passed away on the 1st of November 1991. I was in Listowel to see her the evening before and we had a fairly good chat and laugh. She was always a very outgoing person and enjoyed using modern language, especially the word, "okey doke", when everything was all right. Just before I left the nursing home that evening she asked to see me. I went to the room with Kathleen who said that my mother smiled straight at me and lifted her thumb in a gesture and said, "okey doke, Liam." These were the last words she ever spoke to me in her life. We buried her after requiem mass at Ballydonoghue Church in the old Lislaughtin Abbey cemetery beside my father. Many memories came to me as we laid her to rest, and, just as at my father's funeral, lines from Kavanagh's *In Memory of my Mother* sprang to my mind:

"*And I think of you walking along a headland*
Of green oats in June,
So full of repose, so rich with life-
And I see us meeting at the end of a town
On a fair day by accident, after
The bargains are all made and we can walk
Together through the shops and stalls and markets
Free in the oriental streets of thought."

Independence and Mobility

If a man does not keep pace with his companion, perhaps it is because he hears a different drummer. Let him stop to the music he hears, however measured on way.

(David Thoreau)

A year later, I applied to the Irish Guide Dogs for the blind for a course on mobility training. They visited me at my home, and the mobility instructor took me walking in my local area. He mentioned that I had good balance and remarked that I was carrying a long bamboo stick. I was using this stick to tap the green margins on the side of the road, to guide me. The mobility instructor said, "You have great confidence Liam, but did you ever get into any type of accident?" "Not really", I replied. I explained that potholes and the likelihood of walking into traffic were my greatest fear. He then asked me if I ever left the roadway and got lost. Suddenly my courage dropped, and I explained that I had got lost and had only got back to the road with difficulty. On another occasion I had got lost in a local bog, which I thought I knew very well.

Our walk lasted about an hour and I began to notice that this was a testing time for me. The instructor told me that if I wished to have better mobility, I would have to do an intensive training course. I was offered a preference of doing the course locally, or at the centre near Cork City. I was ashamed to be seen locally with the white cane, so I chose the centre near Cork City. On the morning before leaving to start the course, I was very frightened and apprehensive about the outcome.

I travelled alone by train and thankfully was met at the station by a mobility instructor. It greatly relaxed and cheered me when he greeted me with a firm handshake. He said, "Well done Liam, you made it and you won't regret it".

On arriving at the centre, we toured the residence and were shown the amenities. This consisted of an old two-storey farmhouse, which was converted into single en-suite bedrooms, which were used to accommodate the mobility-training students. It also contained a utility room and recreation room. Lectures and training were conducted in-house to begin with, and progressed to the outer grounds, and later to the main roads. There were about half a dozen students, two for guide dog training and four being taught white cane training skills.

All dressed up and going to a wedding

On the following morning, all students assembled in the recreation area for our first lesson. Punctuality had been impressed on us to accommodate the smooth running of the course. Great emphasis was placed on knocking twice on doors to avoid causing injury to other students. For our benefit, all staff and instructors emphasised that with regard to introductions, that one's first name must be used, i.e. "Good morning Liam, I am John Wade". This is a custom that I personally wish would extend to the sighted community. My first training session that morning was indoors, showing me how to manoeuvre in an upstairs situation. I was walking with my instructor, who stopped suddenly and produced a set of door keys. Shaking them in front of me, he asked me if I recognised them by sound and I answered, "Yes". He threw them away from him, asking at the same time how far away I thought they were and if I could locate them. Confidently, I said, "No problem", and stepped forward to retrieve them. I was about to do so, when suddenly he placed his hand across my chest and called, "Stop". He said, "Do you realise where you are, Liam?" I answered, "in an upstairs room". "Hold my hand" he instructed, saying "step forward, carefully". "One-step more Liam and you would be dead". We were standing at the top of a twenty-foot staircase.

We went down and sat on the bottom step and considered this situation. I was in deep shock, and barely heard his voice when he asked, "Have you ever been frightened before?" Up to then, I was over-confident and had a false image in my mind of my ability to cope in a situation like this, so I explained the serious event that had happened a few months ago. I had been walking home across familiar bog land. I knew this area like the back of my hand, but was unaware that a farmer had opened a new trench. Luckily I fell into this hole feet first and ended up to my hips in bog mould. Just how deep or wide this hole was I could not tell, and in desperation I grabbed the grass on the bank, but it came away with me. The bog was soft, so I was able to dig my hands in deep and dragged myself slowly out. My instructor never mentioned this incident again. "Now you will realise how important this mobility course will be for you". I placed my hand on his shoulder and said, "Thank you". He ended on a light note,

"Go along to the dining room, have a cup of tea and we will meet in an hour's time". This helped to relieve the tension of the past hour.

Our training resumed and one of the first lessons was to learn how to use a white cane correctly. For this lesson, a long rope was used as a guide, winding in and out across the concrete yard. We had to follow this rope keeping in step with our white cane, moving from left to right i.e. left forward, cane at right-hand side, right foot forward, cane on left hand side. This system, when used correctly, made the use of the cane very effective but, before I achieved success, I cursed myself repeatedly for the mistakes I had made. My instructor advised me to practice these lessons at anytime, even after class. One evening during exercise, he asked me if I had any training in marching or obeying commands. I explained that almost thirty-five years ago I had done basic military training at Collin's Barracks, which were a few miles away as the crow flies. "That's amazing after all those years, Liam" he said, "it still shows and is a great help to you now".

As a farmer-countryman they thought it important to teach me how to manoeuvre in an open field. The most amazing piece of equipment I encountered during my training was a battery-operated compass. By holding it against my chest, it would tell me North, South, East or West and the points between. The rectangular field was about four acres and I was taken to the centre. The instructor then asked me how I would find my way from the centre without help. I placed the torch-shaped compass in front of me, moving it until it found the direction North, where I knew the exit gate was located. Slowly I walked in this direction, sometimes wavering, but always relying on my compass to keep me on the right path. Eventually, to my delight and that of my instructor, I placed my hands on the gate. The instructor told me to lean on the gate, rest for a while and enjoy my success.

After ten days of intensive training, we had completed the course. We were then advised not to compare our mobility skills with each other, as our success depended on our own ability, not anybody elses, at all times. Finally the chief instructor congratulated each student and presented her or him with his long white cane. I was homeward bound, but did not fully realise that a whole new world was awaiting me.

After-care mobility training was provided locally so that I could move safely in my own parish. I was very proud of my success to date, so I chose the streets of Knocknagoshel for my first test. It would be here that I would collect my pension, attend church and socialise with my friends. The instructor talked a map through my mind, indicating vital details, such as where to cross the road, the dangerous pavement levels and how to avoid them. He adopted the same procedure when leaving the village.

I was well accustomed to finding my way around the house, if furniture was not moved and kitchen utensils were left in their own place. This caused no inconvenience. I now began to discover here also, that the white cane training was a great help. It also helped to increase my awareness and concentration powers. This training lasted for four days and during this time the instructor lived with us.

One night during my training, my instructor, an Englishman, asked me to go for a drink at the local pub, "The Wounded Knee". During training he had heard the witty language of the locals and wanted to sample the atmosphere of a country pub. Before entering the premises, I asked him what was his usual drink. "Guinness", he replied, "But not more than three half pints". "Only women drink half pints in these parts", I replied. "Order two pints", I said, "and afterwards you can top it up with a half pint and in that way you won't look like a sissy". "I would like to order the first drink", he said. "How would I go about it?" he enquired. "Pull your stool up to the bar, lay your hands on the counter and say two pints there, pints here mean only Guinness". We had nearly emptied our glasses, when the barman recognised my instructor. He had seen him working with me. "As you are the first instructor for the blind to visit this pub, I must stand you a drink" and he smilingly placed two more pints in front of us.

By the end of this pint, my English friend turned to me and said, "This Guinness, as you say, is indeed like mother's milk!" I bought my round and by then the Englishman was listening to stories that were growing ten foot tall by the minute. A song started and though my trainer could not sing, he lifted his glass and joined in the chorus. At closing time we headed for the door. He asked where the gents were. "Over at the back of that tractor", I replied. My instructor called out of the darkness, "This way Liam", "No John", I said, "You are going in the wrong direction". I got the better of the argument when I said, "I know the way home like the back of my hand". As I was holding the cane with one hand, I said, "hang on to my coat and I'll get you home safely". "What if we get lost?" "Then all my training and your instructions will be a disaster". "Oh my God", he murmured.

Half an hour later we arrived home safe and sound and I have never seen a man to go to bed so quickly. The next day he told me he enjoyed the night immensely, but when next he would have a drink, it would be half measures and he would never again touch a pint.

Before leaving, the instructor shook my hand saying, "You are on your own now, good luck, be careful and I am sure you'll be fine".

I was at home one night, and anxious to get to the local so that I could get a comfortable seat. A lady, who was visiting us, noticing my impatience said, "If I were your wife I would murder you, God give me patience". Defiantly, I grabbed my cane and with my newfound confidence, I made my way on my own to the local that was over a mile away. I got a great burst of applause from my friends when they saw me enter our pub, unaided, for the first time in many years. I have had many happy experiences in my life, but this stands out in my memory.

Some years later, the National Council for The Blind made computers available through the Health Board, which were adapted especially for the blind. I was very nervous of modern technology, but thought this was an opportunity too good to pass up. On the advice of my social worker, I placed my application and was thrilled and surprised when it was successful.

The next stage was to find someone to help me to use this machine. My social worker put me in contact with a person who would instruct me on all facets of computers. I was greatly surprised and encouraged when I discovered that this tutor was also blind. For better or worse, I had walked myself into the wonderful world of computers.

My first lesson took place in my own home, which I think made it a lot easier for me. Before starting, my tutor, Toddy Carey explained the benefits of a computer. The first lesson was simple, just learning to switch on the machine, open a programme and most importantly how to shut down and switch off the computer. I had to repeat these exercises until Toddy was sure that I was capable of doing them and that I understood his instructions clearly. How lucky I was that Toddy was blessed with the patience of Job! After about three weeks of operating the computer, Toddy felt that I was capable of starting typing lessons. As this was outside his field, he arranged to have a typist teach me this skill. Of course, it was important that this lady was capable of teaching typing to the blind.

Again, I was lucky that she visited my home for one-to-one tuition. "Typing is a skill", she explained, "That can be perfected by repetition but demands concentration and determination". How right Mary was. In about six weeks or so, I had attained an adequate standard of typing. I sometimes became tired of writing and rewriting, "The quick brown fox jumped over the fence" etc. When I completed this course, the co-coordinator Toddy examined my progress. He was pleased and asked if I would attend a computer course which he was setting up in Tralee. I agreed, but had to discuss this with my wife Kathleen, as there was no public transport out of Knocknagoshel. She encouraged me and said she would provide transport, so I commenced the course. Once it became known that I was attending the class, several neighbours who were working in Tralee offered lifts.

Back to School

"A good objective for a teacher would be to enable those who are doing poorly to do well, and to enable those who are doing well to do better."

(Author unknown)

One morning I was waiting for my drive, when a local farmer stopped and said, "Liam you are going early to the bog". "To the bog", I exclaimed, "No, Joe. Did you not hear that I have returned to college?" He must have heard the news, because he offered me his hand and wished me luck. This meant a lot to me, as he was one of my best friends from farming days

This course progressed and more students who were blind, joined the class. It was becoming obvious to Toddy, that the course should expand and broaden its base. This he planned to do, saying, "All work and no play, makes Jack a dull boy".

Anne Kennelly, who worked in Siamsa Tíre - The National Folk Theatre, came to visit us. She invited us to the theatre, where she interviewed us. Like all the other members, I was shocked when she said that it was her ambition to present a live show, with us blind students performing on the stage with members of the Siamsa Tíre performing company.

On our first day at Siamsa Tíre, we were asked to sit in a horseshoe shape group, while Anne addressed us. Oliver, the Artistic Director, asked us to clap our hands and stamp our feet in rhythm. Oliver hummed a tune and led us in the clapping and stamping. Next step was to stand and move in rhythm. We were not great, but it seemed as if we were doing OK. Anne spoke to each of us individually to find out if we would enjoy doing a performance. My own personal view as I explained then was that I thought it was great fun, but sheer madness. After a month's intense training and preparation, we were ready to present a show, which was called "Tabhair Dom do Lámh" (Give me your hand).

It was an outstanding success and drew an amazing audience of over three hundred people. Apparently, we were the first blind group in Ireland to do such a show and received huge media attention. The success of this show must have moved Anne to join our group as a development co-coordinator. Toddy continued as Chief coordinator, but must have welcomed Anne's input. Another outcome of our success was that we were given bigger and much more suitable accommodation. We all appreciated Anne's work and gave her a warm reception the morning she officially joined our group.

I started learning from Anne on the 14th of February in the year 2000. My typing was not good, but progressing well, although c ompleting a full written sentence was a difficulty for me. Since I had not seen the written word for years, I thought it would be impossible to learn. I pleaded with her to excuse me from this part of the course, but she said, "No. You are well capable of talking, so write down what you have just said. Take no notice of mistakes or spellings. They can be corrected later". This was a great encouragement, so out of sheer devilment, I wrote a letter to my dog. When Anne saw this letter, she thought it was hilarious and suggested that I should continue to write more of these stories.

I progressed sufficiently for Anne to suggest that I start writing a personal learning journal. My first entry into this journal was about my lobbying of politicians to secure a mobility allowance for the blind. I requested of the Kerry County Council, on behalf of the blind community, that a blind mobility allowance be paid to them. I requested the chairman to put the motion on the agenda for the next meeting. He informed me that it would be discussed on the third Monday of March, and he advised me to inform as many councillors as possible. I outlined the case in great detail to each councillor. I believe this was why the motion was successful. This was a very important exercise for me, as I got to know my local representatives and the workings of the Council.

On Monday, the 20th of March 2000, I learned how to install a floppy disc and work on it. This helped me when I did research on holy wells for our next stage production. I found that the floppy disc could be used for many projects.

My next learning experience was learning to receive and send e-mails. I was very pleased with this exercise, as I was able to communicate with my many friends around the world at the press of a button. I got a lot of enjoyment from this, trying to explain, how a blind person could operate a computer. Writing these e-mails also helped me to properly construct sentences and to improve my spelling.

The interaction with other blind people of different ages and backgrounds has helped me to understand life better. I had been blind for over twenty years and did not have the pleasure of reading letters or replying to them. I have now learned how to operate a scanner, which reads all my letters, and stores them for further reference. I will never forget the day I had a letter read out to me by the voice on my computer. Learning to type and send letters to my friends was wonderful, telling them that I had gone back to school to learn more about computers. It was lovely to hear their praise and encouragement to continue with this wonderful opportunity. I am enjoying the learning course and will continue until I have completed my education.

We presented our show "Tabhair Dom Do Lámh" again at Siamsa Tíre on April 25th. It was a great experience for me to meet and renew my acquaintance with the members of Siamsa Tíre. I was surprised at how much I had forgotten from last year's performance. As soon as the music started and I heard the singing of Sabrina and Tom, it all came back to me and I regained my confidence. I enjoyed working with the other blind people on the show, and hearing from them and what the show meant to them. One thing I learned to do, was to follow the sound of a particular bodhrán, played by a member of Siamsa Tíre. This was very good training and did a lot to help my mobility when walking the streets.

We all enjoyed participating in the show with Siamsa Tíre and got a standing ovation from the audience. Later, we decided that we should make a presentation to Siamsa Tíre in honour of the occasion. After some research, we decided on something appropriate and chose to present them with a scroll. I was very pleased when I was asked by the group to make the presentation. I was very nervous when I started to speak to such a professional group, but I soon got confidence by using the Irish language for my introduction. I thanked Siamsa Tíre on behalf of our group for their work and dedication in presenting the show. I then presented the scroll to Anne Kennelly, who accepted it on behalf of Siamsa Tíre. Martin Whelan, Manager, replied on behalf of the Siamsa Tíre Company and said what a wonderful experience it was for them to have worked with the blind community. He thanked our group for the scroll and said it would always be there to remind them of this occasion. In conclusion, he promised the full support of the Company and help for future projects.

One day in June 2000, Kathleen and I received another very generous offer from our Australian cousin Peter Gray, to holiday with him in Australia, all expenses paid. In late September, we started on the first leg of our journey from Shannon to Heathrow Airport. Everything was going well, until we arrived in Heathrow, when a security officer who asked me for my passport confronted me. He studied the passport very carefully, before asking

Kathleen and I to accompany him to a private office. He looked sharply at me, asking if I was really blind. I explained that I was, but he still insisted on examining my white cane. Having done so, he handed it back to me, saying, "Good luck and enjoy your holiday". I realise that my eyes give the impression of good sight and this may have caused the confusion. I was not surprised when the same situation occurred again at Bangkok Airport.

Our cousin Peter met us at Sydney Airport and escorted us to his home, where we stayed for the duration of our holiday. We went on daily excursions and Peter also gave us tickets for the main events at the Olympic Games. All this was very exciting, but also made me aware of the effort Kathleen had to make to cope for two people in a strange environment.

One morning, as we were preparing to visit the outback, Kathleen received a call from Ireland. I was aware from her silence that something was wrong, and before she finished the call, she handed the phone to me. It was from my brother-in-law, telling me that my brother Patrick had suffered a very serious accident and was not expected to live. Three days later my niece phoned us to say that my brother had died.

It was a very upsetting time for us, and being so far away from home, we missed the support of our family, so we decided to return home immediately. Our Australian relatives were very understanding and gave us every possible support.

They saw us off at Sydney Airport and the cabin staff on the plane, and captain, also showed great sympathy and understanding. This helped us to endure the long journey home. At the request of the captain, we were given a bottle of the finest Australian wine. The Captain offered his condolences and said, "I hope you will return to Australia again, but in the meantime keep this bottle and celebrate when times are better". We arrived back very tired, and just in time to escort my brother's remains back to his home for a traditional wake.

The following day, his body was taken to Church for the celebration of Mass. Afterwards, the people expressed their sympathy and Patrick was laid to rest next to his son, Elton. Elton had died of a brain haemorrhage, just twelve months previously, R.I.P. Patrick's daughter, Aidín, gave the eulogy at the graveside, describing the life of a lovely brother and wonderful father. Some weeks later, my tutors from the Braille and I.T. class in Tralee contacted me and asked me to return to school in my own time.

When I returned to school, I discovered that my tutor, Anne, had started a fitness class at the Sports Complex. This encouraged us to use rowing machines, treadmills and body exercising equipment. My tutor asked if I could swim. "No", I replied. "Well we are not going to throw you in at the deep end, but would you be prepared to give it a try Liam?" she asked. I did give it a try and started taking instructions from Mary Mc Donnell. She told me that learning to hold my breath with my head under water was very important. After some weeks, we progressed to the open pool and made headway, even learning to swim under water. I continued to take instruction, until I was able to swim across the pool unaided.

On July 9th 2001, our tutor Anne, asked us to prepare ourselves for abseiling on a cliff near Killarney. We walked to the top of a Cliff, where trained instructors from Cappanalea Outdoor Education Centre met us. My instructor checked my harness for safety and took every precaution to ensure that I was fit, in mind and body, for descending fifty metres of a sheer cliff face. We went over the cliff together, attached by a rope through a ring, which would ease out as I lowered myself into a horizontal position. I descended cautiously, making sure my feet were firmly on the cliff-face at all times, before moving on. I was thrilled when the instructor told me that I was only about ten feet from the ground, but warned me that I must still be very careful. It was great to touch the ground again, but my God what a thrill it was to have completed this operation successfully.

The next part of our outdoor pursuit programme involved a canoeing trip for the group on Caragh Lake, near the town of Killorglin. I was very excited at this prospect, as I had never gone canoeing or sailing previously. We had to wear life jackets and were shown how to use them. Our gear included helmets, wellington boots and all-weather outdoor suits. The instructors showed us how to use a paddle, with one person at each end of the canoe. The instructors then rowed to the centre of the lake. They called on us to row in their direction. As a help to finding them, the instructors started bleating like sheep and we rowed in their direction.

When we got near them, we were told to bark like dogs, then the instructors scattered in all directions, with us in hot pursuit.

The idea was that each canoe crew should place a paddle on an instructor's boat, indicating a capture for us. Finally, after about an hour's pursuit and great fun, all the pursuing canoes had captured a boat and claimed it as a prize. We all agreed that this exercise had been successful and, without knowing it, we were all gaining greater knowledge of mobility. I believe this was the real purpose of the exercise.

Abseiling at Gap of Dunloe, Killarney June 6, 2003

Next we completed a basic cooking course and a food hygiene programme. We were then presented with certificates at a ceremony at the Institute of Technology in Tralee town. The use of a talking microwave oven has helped me greatly, and relieved my dear wife of some of the drudgery in the kitchen!

Our level of fitness had reached a very high peak, so our tutor Anne Kennelly thought it time to introduce us to a new game called goal ball. This is a version of football, designed especially for the visually impaired. To be able to identify the ball when moving, it makes a special ringing sound. As a group, we decided to call ourselves the Kerry Goalballers and we all got green and gold jerseys with that logo. It is a three-a-side game, with a fullback and two corner backs. Before starting any game, our physical training instructor, Pat Flanagan, put us through the most rigorous exercise I have ever experienced. The playing area is about the size of a badminton court, well marked for the benefit of the referee. Each team knelt, then lined out taking up positions at opposite ends of the court, kneeling on mats in a letter A formation. We started by rolling the ball on the ground towards the opposite team, who had to stop or catch the ball, and return it to us calling our names to let us know it was coming back. If at any time the ball went over the end line, that counted as a goal.

We practiced this routine for several weeks, before we had an actual competitive game. Our referee for our first important game was our tutor, Anne Kennelly.

Before starting, she read out the rules, stating that she would tolerate no nonsense! However, during the game she gave a decision she had to reverse. We told her that it was a good job that she was not refereeing the World Cup, or she would cause more trouble than Roy Keane. The game was played in a sporting manner and it looked as if a draw would be a good result. Then I heard our fullback Aodán O Conchúir calling, "Ball coming fast on your right, Liam". I dived and caught it, but somehow the ball went under my arm and over the line for a winning goal. I cursed and swore and tried to retrieve it, but sadly for our team the green flag had gone up.

I protested to the referee that the goal should be disallowed and that she should declare the game a draw. "I heard you use bad language Liam and any more noise out of you, and I will give you a red card". "For goodness sake, Anne" I protested. Then she showed me the red card and to the applause of both teams, and to my amusement, I was sent to the side-line. After some weeks playing this game, I noticed while walking with the aid of my white cane, that my awareness on the streets had become much more focused and sharper.

Guide Dog

Man's best friend and what a friend he proved to be….

(the author)

One morning, I was walking briskly up the familiar route in Tralee town, aided by my white cane and concentrating deeply. Then I heard a familiar voice calling, "Move over a little Liam". It was my tutor Toddy. He passed me by swiftly and I became aware, that he had a guide dog. I was amazed that he was so mobile with the aid of a dog. I was aware that Toddy owned one, but had never encountered him, or any guide dog in action. Later, when entering the school, Toddy made a joke about my slow pace in comparison to his fast progress. He called me aside and asked if I had ever thought of applying for a dog. "They're a wonderful help, and great company. I would strongly advise you to apply and see if you'd qualify. Although I have given my advice, you must remember that the final decision must be yours and yours only".

Following my application, an officer from the guide dog centre visited our home to interview me and my wife Kathleen. Both of our views were taken into consideration, with great emphasis placed on the fact that the dog would have to live as a close companion to me, and would have to live within the home. Kathleen was apprehensive about having a dog inside permanently, but agreed that if it would help me, that I should go for it. Kathleen asked who would groom and take care of the dog. The trainer replied that I would be taught how to take care of the dog and it would by my responsibility. He also assessed our sheep dog's temperament and his health.

Our boundaries and lands were assessed for suitability. The next thing he did was to attach a dog lead to his arm and together we walked along the road, with me holding onto the lead and with him acting the part of the dog. He gave me commands, such as, "Stop" or "Go". Occasionally, he moved to the left or to the right, checking how quickly I could react. Before leaving, he explained that he couldn't promise anything yet, but he would get back to me. "This is only a preliminary test Liam", he said, "But there will be a further test, should you be considered. In that event, you will have a harder examination to come at the centre in Cork". About two weeks later I received the call and presented myself at the guide dog centre.

My new instructor attached a harness to his body, giving me an attached strap and telling me to treat him as if he were the dog. I was told to give commands as when to go or to stop. On a count of five, I said, "Go" and I followed, moving slowly, through a difficult obstacle course. Each time we repeated this test we were moving faster. Finally, he suggested that I should meet him in his office. There was one other man there, who informed me that I had passed the test. The gentleman then told me that he was pleased with my progress, but the most important thing was to find a suitable dog for my situation. When I asked how long it would take to locate such a dog, he answered, "Just be ready Liam. We can't be certain, but a suitable one will come at some stage", and added that the usual waiting time was between twelve and eighteen months.

I was anxiously awaiting a call from them when, one morning, the phone rang and I was asked would I be at home all day. Later on that day, a lady arrived in a van and came into the house with a lovely Labrador dog. This was to be a test of the dog's temperament and also to check our working speeds. I have a long stride and a quick pace. It would be necessary for the dog to match this pace without tiring. She took me walking with the dog in full harness and told me that she had another lead attached to the dog for safety. We walked for about half a mile, stopping at intervals, discussing what I thought of our progress. She continued to encourage the dog with words, such as "Good boy, good boy". Further discussions took place between the trainer and Kathleen, to assess my wife's attitude to having a dog as a permanent household resident. She next acquainted herself with our sheep dog, Shep. She spent some time talking to him and then returned inside and said, "O.K". Before leaving, she told me to be prepared at any time to come to the centre for training.

Surprisingly, the call came on the same day as we were presenting our show, "Cos, Cos

Eile…" at Siamsa Tíre. It all entailed a bit of a rush, as I had to travel to Cork by public transport immediately after the show.

This was to be a three-week course with my prospective guide dog. I had already missed a full day's training due to my decision to participate in the performance, so I had to start immediately to catch up with the other students. As this was a new purpose-built building, none of my past experience was of any benefit to me. The mobility officer took great care to show me the layout. It was important that I could negotiate around the building without my white cane. I managed this task in a very short time to his satisfaction. "Well done," he said, "This makes my task and yours a lot easier. Where did you learn this mobility?" I explained that we had done classroom mobility training with our tutor, Anne Kennelly, in our training centre.

Roy Keane caught between two Kerry men Liam and his reliable friend Johnny Morrissey, Gortroe, Knocknagashel

At nine o'clock the next morning, a lady handed over a Labrador dog to me. "This is your guide dog, Liam, and his name is Yale". I was then taught how to groom, care for and feed my dog. Great emphasis was placed on continuing with the toilet training that he had already undergone. It was impressed upon me that it was absolutely necessary to have this dog living closely with me, sleeping, eating and being at my heel at all times. It took Yale a few days to befriend me. I was new to him and it would take the dog a little time to get used to me. One morning, I awoke with a slight sneeze and found Yale's wet nose beneath my sheet, sniffing as if to say "Good morning Liam". I put out my hand and stroked him and was aware of his wagging tail. I knew we had bonded.

I eventually passed all the tests and was given my dog. I paid fifty pence - the purchase price for him. Perhaps our last important lesson was being told that there was no such thing as the perfect guide dog, and no perfect owner. We were told to remember that at all times it would be a joint effort. The dog would be our eyes; we must use our ears, and take care.

We returned home and importantly the instructor introduced our sheep dog, to my guide dog. She insisted that they meet outside the house, making sure that Yale had accepted Shep's senior position as leader. Fortunately, to date, things have worked out well.

Yale has become a wonderful companion and has made many friends for me on my travels. We have visited schools and hospitals to raise awareness of what it is like to be blind. The children love Yale and it is very rewarding to hear the appreciation of the aged in their wards, as they stroke and pet my dog. I have a great sense of pride and independence when I go to collect my pension in Knocknagoshel, or walk the streets of Tralee with the aid of my guide dog Yale.

On the second week, training took us onto a main road, and I will never forget the fear of the noise of the approaching traffic. I gave Yale the commands that I had been taught and as he started to walk forward confidently, these fears quickly left me. There were times during this intensive course, that I felt incapable of continuing. Thanks to the instructors whose

With my guide dog Yale at the Braille class at I.T.class Tralee.

help was always at hand, I did not fail. Before I went blind, I had been a serious collector of rare, historical books. The leather binding on the Dublin produced books was more important to me than the actual contents. When my sight started to fail, I stopped collecting these rare items. However, after some time, my sense of touch and judgement had so improved, that I started collecting them again. It is due to this hobby, that I made contact and deep friendship with many like-minded collectors from all parts of Ireland. Over the phone, we talked and discussed all aspects of book-collecting.Finding rare editions unexpectedly was a great thrill.

If I found two editions of a rare book, it would be possible to exchange one of these items with another collector, who might have more than one edition of another rare book. To this day, book collecting remains my favourite hobby and it brings great joy, when young students call to my house to do research.

I remember 2003 as being a very important year in Kerry, as we celebrated one hundred years of the V.E.C.'s contribution to education in the county. I am sure every one would agree that for our blind students, their proudest moment was when we were asked to perform our latest stage show called, "Deir me, Deir tú..." (I say, You say), before the President of Ireland, Mary McAleese. We were the first blind group to perform for any president of Ireland. We received great acclaim from the media for this production.

With my friends on stage at Siamsa Tíre following our performance of "Deir mé, Deir tú" March 2003

The Beat of the Bodhrán

Dance, dance, dance to the beat
Sing songs of life bitter sweet
On the stage of Siamsa Tíre we laugh and cheer
Our nerves are on edge, and we are full of fear
The beat of the Bodhrán as the beat of our hearts
Urging us on as we dance in the dark

When the blind of Kerry appear on stage
With music and rhythm they dance and they play
A story unfolds, they are seeds very small
Laying still on the ground with no movement at
all
Till the sun warms the Earth and they grow into
flowers
And trees that sway in the breeze for hours and
hours

As the music erupts, feet tap to the beat,
Song echo round the hall and into the street
Emotions are high as the curtain falls
And with tears in their eyes the audience
applaud
For the music let them see and dance made them
free
Hearts full of joy even though they could not see

When I first went blind, I feared that I would lose my identity in the community and I could see myself doing nothing except spending most of my time listening to a radio. The wonderful technology of the computer age has opened a whole new world for me. With the aid of a computer, I have made friends from many parts of the world. Each week I send and receive e-mails about diverse topics, including politics and new aids for the blind, which are coming on stream almost daily.

But of all these letters and e-mails, the one I remember most was the one I wrote and posted to my wife. It was her first letter from me for forty years, thanking Kathleen for all her understanding and kindness shown me over the years.

Through the eyes of my friends I will always see.

Liam

POSTSCRIPT

Evaluation of 'Súile le Solas'

The theme of 'Súile le Solas' - living life by the light of my heart - means for me, a person who once had sight, a re-awakening of a dormant part of my brain to see once again the countryside that I enjoyed in my youth; the movement of farm animals and wild-life, and to picture again the human faces I had thought lost to memory.

Over a period of time in 2001, all the blind students in Tralee came together to create a collage. We were asked to recollect and reflect upon a particular part of our sighted life, and to come up with an idea or design that we could create manually to symbolise it. I recalled working in the fields with horses as a young man, and the great delight I took in closing in the earth over wheat grains with a rolling stone and the smooth levelling effect this had on a field. Having created the wheat garden in my mind, I designed a rolling stone. Handling the materials for the collage showed me the great use I had of my hands. Having completed the wheat garden and rolling stone, I believed that I could work with more and more materials, creating images of other scenes from my sighted days. The idea of this being made into a collage in the shape of an Ogham Stone, and the contribution of other students in the class with their views of what they had seen, and for the blind who had never seen, through our collective ideas, made up a wonderful picture of a living world.

The picture was all the more complete when each student made an individual piece and, for me, making a rolling stone and a wheat garden, meant that my contribution blended in perfectly with those of the other students to complete the picture of a living life. Having handled the materials, I felt a renewal of the feeling of life into my hands once more, a wonderful feeling indeed. Working on it, at the start, seemed a bit ambitious, but, as I succeeded, it was a sheer delight as my task was completed. I have feared failure since I went blind, but working on this project with my fellow students has given me great confidence, and, from conversations with the other students, they had the same experience.

Life as I know it, starts in the morning with the sun and ends in the evening with the sunset, that's what I felt with this collage. The idea of taking this collage to the Siamsa Tíre group and giving them an insight into our world, so that both worlds, the world of the sighted and the visually impaired, could express this idea in drama, dance, music and mime, breathed life into our collage work. It gave meaning to our project.

I felt that having laboured together on the collage piece, we had a certain confidence and sureness when collaborating with the Siamsa Tíre group in the workshops. I was pleased to note that during the very early parts of the workshop, each student, myself included, could confidently explain the meaning of our work and the show that we were about to produce. It was very new to me to have to describe colour, because I have known colour in my sighted years which are only a memory now. But I can certainly say that at the end of these workshops I truly knew the difference between red and black, and that's for sure.

Colour in the inner eye of a blind person is a wonderful image and I am privileged to have experienced it, and delighted that this project has reinforced this beautiful part of life in my mind's eye. It is a bit emotional for me to write about this, but the feeling is truly wonderful.

Movement is a very special part of my life, and I was confident of my ability to move through crowded streets and countryside, but, until I participated in these workshops, I was almost unaware that there was great movement all around me. Participating in the workshops has broadened my horizons and has given me a better insight into the life that we share with every other person, a moving, expanding world. When I go to the sea-side again, and hear the laughter of children, the rolling of the ocean, the cries of the sea-birds, I will now know that I am no longer living in a still and static world, everything is moving all around me and I am part of it. Before this, I thought that only I moved and that everything else stood still, and if this project has done anything for me, it has broadened my horizons, and yet brought me back to live in the real world again.

I listened on the radio and TV to the horrors of Sept. 11th. and the terrible consequences for the people as a result of this tragedy. We simulated a scene in the workshop of the plane crashing into the Twin Towers. One student was standing with his hands outstretched, simulating the plane, just about to crash into the towers. We were searching in the rubble for the dead, and this exercise renewed the intense feelings I have for tragedies, and even for love. This emotional experience has helped me to greatly understand myself and these responses and responsibilities in life. Sharing these experiences with sighted people and seeing them having the same response, gives me to understand that the loss of my eyesight does not mean that I do not have a common bond with sighted people.

For half an hour before the Siamsa Tíre performance was due to begin, I felt a groundswell of emotion in my being. I had feelings of great courage and anxiety, but, then I heard my friend and classmate, Tom Brosnan, starting off on his own playing 'Eanach Dhúin' on his mouth organ, and my pride and my confidence came straight to the fore. Placing my hands on another blind student, and starting to walk on to the stage in the chain was a wonderful support. Now the game was on, and all fear was gone, let your heart and soul go Liam, you have twenty minutes to win the hearts and open the minds of the audience. I felt as light as a bird in the air and each part of the performance came to me with a sense of ease so that I did not have to think of what I was doing. I was truly enjoying myself.

As I started to perform on the day, I recalled to my mind the words of my late brother, Pádraig, during our first performance, 'Tabhair Dom Do Lámh', when he said with pride and tears in his eyes: 'That's my brother Liam, that's performing'. The tears came almost to my eyes, but I held back because an old proverb came to my mind: 'Whatever happens, the show must go on'. All through the show, I heard my brother's voice saying: 'That's my brother, Liam', and when we took our bow at the end of the show, I said aloud, but it could not be heard in the surge of applause: 'This one was for you, Paddy'.

I have participated in the three 'Hidden Voices' shows and each experience is a complete renewal of confidence, still a challenge, but, with my experience I am now looking forward to taking part in a new project next year. I feel the benefits of taking part in these shows are wonderful for me, personally. I am the only unsighted person in my extended family, and having the family come to these performances has created an even deeper bond and understanding between them and me.

At one stage, they all felt sorry for me because I lost my sight. This has now turned to a sense of pride. As they all say, I've become a more colourful personality and their sorrow for me has now turned to admiration. I've even heard my own nephews and nieces of a new generation say that they have taken an inspiration from my work, and from my way of life. I certainly believe that this would not have happened without my participation in the Braille I.T. programme, but especially not without these shows, where they can see me participate in real life. One of them in particular, my niece, told me that when she feels down in life, all she has to do to help her is to think of what I have achieved. It gives me a wonderful feeling to know that I, through my participation, can be of help to them.

I also feel that I can now participate better with them socially when I go out to have a pint and a singsong with them. I have joined their way of life and can discuss mobile phones, theatre, the wonderful world of computers and the internet with them. My social and communication skills have improved immensely, and this has helped me to keep in contact with my many friends and relations around the world.

Reflection on 'Cé tusa istigh?' (Who Are You Inside)

Ever since I went blind, I tried to hide from my own mind, the things that caused me great worry. Part of my mind held the strange moments in my life close to the surface, ready for recall. I lived life and tried to hold back on the dark sides of my own personality. In short, I was becoming more and more a stranger to myself. Even my wife and very closest friends were unaware of this great change. Hidden flashes from past experiences sometimes surfaced at the strangest of moments. This could happen walking the road, in church, or worst of all, in my deep dreams.

I knew that it was particularly soul destroying and damaging for me. Trying to brush it aside when in the company of friends made me change my personality. I would automatically change the subject to a more frivolous story. Unable to recognise the features of another human being, also left me unaware of their thinking. At this point in time, I liked to touch and feel sculptures or works of art that would remind me of past events.

That sense of remoteness was worst when I realised that I would never again recognise the faces of my friends, or my own vision, in a mirror. I will never forget the day when our tutor, Anne Kennelly, told us we could make moulds of our own faces. Most of the men in our group had completed their moulds sooner than I. Through these images, and to my great delight, I began to recognise the faces of my classmates. With the help of the others I completed my own mask. It was very rewarding for me the day I recognised the mask of my own face from the masks of the others on the table. In short, my eyes were being opened in the real sense, into a very strange and unusual world. This was the first part of the preparations for our performance of 'Cé tusa istigh?'

The first change for me was that I began to recognise that the kernel of my real problem was my sense of isolation and remoteness. I knew that I would have to reach deep into my heart and my soul to put meaning and a clearer expression on my mask. To really understand myself, I had to walk back into my memory, walk the streets of my local village and experience my feelings. With this work completed, I brought my ideas to class and shared them with my other classmates. Their individual stories differed from mine, and their experiences in life differed somewhat from what was tormenting me. However, when I listened to my classmates and heard their stories, a fuller picture of the life of a blind person began to form. All the parts of our unusual experiences began to mingle and we knew we had a very important story to tell.

The great change in my mind commenced when I began to reveal myself clearly to my tutor and the class. This, I believed, was the foundation for me gaining new strength and composure. I remember clearly when I used to hide my thoughts from my friends and tell a frivolous story. Now, I was telling the truth and seeing myself as I had never done before. This indeed, was hard work, but my God, was it worthwhile.

The next major task for me, and my fellow students, was to work out how we would communicate these feelings to the public. We worked together for months, preparing and bringing our show together. This involved all of us identifying a situation in life where these feelings came to the fore, developing that situation to the point where it could convey our messages to the audience.

For the first time since I went blind, I found a new use for my white cane. We tapped out the rhythms of our show with our canes, alerting the minds of the audience to the message we were going to bring. As I stood on the stage that day, something within me brought fear to my soul. The fear was that, at long last, I was going to expose my true self to the wider audience.

But, as the show progressed, and the other students started to tell their stories, a certain sense of pride broke within my heart. For I now knew that the people in the audience would understand me and that I would understand myself. I can truly and honestly say that, in those few minutes that I performed on the stage, all that great sense of hidden fear started to vanish.

Over the six years of participating in the 'Hidden Voices From the Dark' project, I've grown in confidence with each phase. But, the one thing that had remained in my mind until our performance day this year, was that awful sense of sadness, isolation and remoteness. Having revealed my inner thoughts and cleansed my mind of these feelings, I now feel a much happier and freer person.

The Road to Starrey's Cross

Composed by Johnny Morrissey
Gortroe, Knocknagoshel.

When I was young and innocent, I thought I'd like to roam
Like many another foolish lad, I had no thoughts of home
My parents' kind I left behind, not thinking of my loss
And the home I knew in sweet Gortroe, a mile from Starrey's cross.

By the Glena stream, we dreamed our
dreams, as we went where youngsters go
We roamed about and fished for trout, in the
valley down below
O'er Cummer hill and rippling rill, we
tramped to school and Mass
From the homes we knew down in Gortroe,
just west of Starrey's Cross

By the quarry gate, when the night was late,
we hurried with our fears
For inside we knew were a motley crew, the
ghosts of many years
On foot or bike, we made a hike; beneath us
grew no grass
And when out alone, we sprinted home, on the
road from Starrey's Cross.

In my minds eye, I can see that sky, as the sun
sinks towards the sea
While standing still on a Kerry hill, in the
townland of Muingwee
From the rolling plain around Moyvane, to
the lofty height of Meen
From Cnocanore to Tuareenmore, what a
splendid scenic dream.

Then turning east my eyes I feast, on the lights of Abbey town
That sparkle in the twilight, when the evening Sun goes down
Towards Brosna and Mountcollins and on to Seacongloss
I can see them still, from Sheehy's Hill, on the road to Starrey's Cross.

Now strangers lands are great to see and strangers sometimes kind
But there are none so dear to me, as the friends I left behind
And when I see a jet plane stream, beneath the Southern Cross
I sigh and moan and pine for home and the road to Starrey's Cross.

And now dear friends it is time to go, forgive me my lament
My bones are getting weary knowing my years are nearly spent
And all I ask from heaven above, when on my way I pass
That my soul might roam, round my old home and the road to Starrey's Cross.

*"My heart will always be at home in my town-
land of Gortroe."*

(Liam)

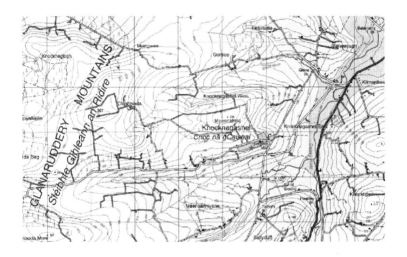

With every true friendship, we build more firmly the foundations on which the peace of the whole World rests.

(Mahatma Gandhi)

*Enjoying a cup of tea with my good friend
Larry Keane and the President of Ireland*